RESILIENT

MASCOT®
B O O K S
an imprint of Amplify Publishing Group

www.amplifypublishinggroup.com

Resilient: A Story of Group Home Survival

For more information, please contact:
Mascot Books, an imprint of Amplify Publishing Group
620 Herndon Parkway, Suite 220
Herndon, VA 20170
info@mascotbooks.com

Library of Congress Control Number: 2023924182
CPSIA Code: PRV0424A
ISBN-13: 978-1-63755-946-8

Cover artwork by Luca James-Felt

Printed in the United States

This memoir is dedicated to my beautiful, brilliant, and amazing wife, Shauna. You kept me from losing myself to a darkness that was pulling apart my soul, gave me a purpose I never knew I needed, and showed me what real love feels like. I would not be the man I am today if not for you, my love, and this book would never have been published.

A STORY OF
GROUP HOME SURVIVAL

MASCOT
BOOKS
an imprint of Amplify Publishing Group

RESILIENT
JEREMY BRACAMONTES

CONTENTS

This is a true story. One of survival and of resiliency.

———

"Fall seven times, get up eight. *Nana korobi, ya oki.*"
—JAPANESE PROVERB

PROLOGUE

─────────

The true character of a society is revealed
in how it treats its children.

—NELSON MANDELA

I felt a gentle touch from the sun. An intoxicating heat nestled close to my face.

It was a warm promise that floated around me and assured me everything was okay. The perfect weather and a butter-soft breeze rocked my drooping brown eyes into a fantastic, head-bobbing slumber. My old car seat held me in a comforting embrace, and I felt safe.

I remember my father's long black hair blowing around the headrest, his left arm resting over the leather steering wheel and leaning along the open window bay. The smooth air smelled of exhaust fumes, trees, cigarettes, and my mother's perfume. He was a strong Latino and had his other arm wrapped around my mother, who leaned in close. He was her protector.

Then my fantasy world became stagnant on dark hinges. Peace and safety evaporated.

That welcoming dream ended, and a vivid nightmare began with horrific screeching from my father's red Mercury Cougar. He slammed desperately on squeaking brakes and arched his broad back in terrible pain. Old tires burned their rubber on the hot pavement, and it smelled awful. His agonized screams and face crushed by anguish haunted my dreams.

Dramatic visions of that scene captured my senses and ran repetitively through my destroyed heart. Intense and raw, their gripping power ransacked my soul, squeezing it to nothing. I felt frost cover the warmth of my innocence, and a potent reality darkly awoke.

My youthful father fought lymphoma, in excruciating pain, and lost the war in May 1986.

That horrid disease decimated his power to endure, and he left behind a curly-haired five-year-old boy, with a mourning, heroin-addicted mother. She was lost inside a merciless world of tar and journeyed with her son on a boiling, drug-induced dark fantasy that ended in true loss.

So the story of a lost young boy and survival began . . .

CHAPTER 1

CANCER

Anaheim, California, 1985–1986

———————

*When someone has cancer, the whole family and
everyone who loves them does to.*

—TERRI CLARK

Toxic smells of ether and ammonia rushed toward me like a vast wall of water. The deceitful sliding-glass doors reflected blue as my heart jumped into my throat. They opened toward their steel shells on the outer wall of the cement-colored hospital. Cool air flowed on invisible currents that rushed up from the ground and into my pale face, making me blink.

Overcast clouds slowly sauntered their nomadic journey across the heavens and grimly reflected off the dark mirrored glass of the buildings surrounding the hospital. I felt fear's bony fingers grasping at my soul, peeking through an onyx veil that crackled with desperation.

I was tightly hugging on to my mother's white jean pants as we were dragged into the abominable domain of the dead. Her nervous hand was resting softly on the back of my neck, and I felt her fingers unconsciously playing with the curls at the base of my head. She trembled and was hesitant in her movements. I knew this had to do with my dying father. I had not seen him since the car accident, and this was the first time a hospital visit was not for me.

We swiftly navigated through the crowded foyer of mustard-colored couches full of the sick. There was nobody to escort us up to my father's room; nobody wanted us there. We were the Bracamontes family home-wreckers, the destroyers of a happy life my dad had before us.

Moments at Griffith Park in Los Angeles during the hottest months of summer were hazy. Water-balloon fights, jungle gyms, and barbecues towered over the isolation my mother held us in. We sat by ourselves under a faraway tree that had a canopy so dense we could disappear into the shadows of the branches. Across the park, the Bracamontes clan were loud and rowdy, but we were quiet. We hid in plain sight, and I was not invited to play with the other kids. My father's family was extensive, and we were an unfortunate anomaly that didn't belong. It was pity that allowed this view in the first place.

These glimpses were few, and my dad kept us away from that world. Then he ended up in the hospital.

A thin pathway of people opened before us like maleficent clouds that break apart to reveal a bright moon. The path wound next to a small stand selling artisanal coffee, wafting aromas that reminded me of how much my dad loved bear claws. Sugar-hinted memories sneaked around the fog of my mind, and I saw a glimpse of him happy, free from pain.

He ripped the glazed morsels in half, dunked them in his milky coffee, and always made a glorious mess. Crumbs would tumble all over his shirt and in his handlebar mustache, with coffee dripping down his chin. His crooked smile made it funny, and I felt my crooked smile taking form at the memory.

"Mommy, can I have a bear claw?" I whispered, not knowing why.

She shook her head no and picked me up. "No, mijo, I am sorry." She was shaking, and her gorgeous curly brown hair shivered with her.

I nestled into her neck, and the rhythmic motions calmly rocked me into a bouncing sleep. Another smell overpowered the lingering ether, tenderly touching my nose, and I knew it well: my dad's favorite meal, bacon and eggs.

A powerful vision exploded in my mind. *We were eating breakfast at Norms Diner, with me cuddled up next to my dad. He said to me in a deep voice laced with a Hispanic accent, "Jeremy, mijo, watch me. Eat this way. Aqui, aqui."*

He then scooped a mound of fluffy scrambled eggs onto his fork while grasping a piece of bacon with his other hand and ate it all at once. He then grabbed his strawberry-slathered toast and jammed a bite in his already overloaded mouth, then looked at me with that awesome crooked smile.

"Now you try it, mijo," he mumbled through a mouth full of goodness.

I tried it and succeeded at both, overloading my mouth and getting food all over my lap. He was laughing so hard he fell into the U-shaped seat of the red-leather booth. His infectious laughter made me giggle uncontrollably, and afterward I sat in the crook of his arm, feeling completely safe, completely loved.

Descending back into chaos, my head bounced me awake.

My mother weaved us unsteadily toward the back of the lowly lit hospital lobby, and there was a floating darkness that embodied the few people around us. We met a beautiful Hispanic nurse, with bright red lipstick and perfectly white tennis shoes.

She wore a short-sleeve baby-blue hospital smock that matched her pants and had penetrating brown eyes that held pain. My mother must have known her because they hugged after putting me down. They walked with me between them, speaking in very hushed tones. We emerged into a gray antechamber without windows. The silence was so thick that their whispers felt deafening.

This was a staging area to put on protective clothing, and the lights were so bright I had to squint to look up at my mother. My heart clenched, fear pulsated from my hands into my head, and I knew something bad was happening.

Dull blue shoe coverings matched my baggy scrubs, and my little soles created soft scraping sounds on the freshly waxed linoleum floor. The nurse, who gently dressed me, never dropped her hand from around my shoulder and kept repeating, "It's going to be okay, mijo. You are such a brave little man."

Another mysterious cavity opened before me, leading down a hallway with shiny wallpaper depicting pictures of birds or some type of animal. The pretty nurse was urging my mother forward by placing a hand on her lower back. A comical man in a worker's jumpsuit was coming from the other direction, pushing a cart filled with linens and danced to the beat in his head. He lifted his eyes, winked at me and said, "Órale, mijo."

At the end of the patterned hall was a steel structure that emitted a very low humming sound, and the calming nurse pushed a square button on the wall, which began to glow a neon-ginger color. She knelt and ruffled my hair, with concern etched deeply in her eyes.

There was no music in the gray-carpeted elevator, just the almond-eyed nurse and my devastated mother. She was trancelike, and her clammy hand limply grasped mine. The elevator smelled like old people and boiled vegetables; I wanted to gag. The nurse seemed oblivious to the odor, but my mom had a crinkle in her nose, which could only come from the noxious scent.

The high-pitched ding disturbed the silence as we reached our designated floor. The abrupt stop quickly reminded me that my ailing father was close by in pain. We slowly walked into another area that looked like everything else, and my mother was told to sign the visitors' form at the nurses' station.

A paralyzing dread caused me to squeeze between my mother's legs. From the safety of that barrier, I saw my dad's room at the end of the long hallway. My uncles Dennis and Danny were standing outside the room, looking toward me with an aching sadness. They did not attempt to take me from my timid mother as we approached. Instead, they stared at her, almost like her mere presence was wrong.

The engaging commotion around my father's room intensified as we entered. I did not know any of the people in that sea of faces. Through their baleful gazes, however, it was their disdain for my mother that created animosity. Everyone I walked past either played with my hair or squeezed my little shoulder, and I was somehow untangled from my mother's warm embrace.

Two windows glowed lightly, bathing the area with late-day ambiance. The clouds seemed lower in the sky and had a faint tint of gray, promising evening showers. Their rapid movement resembled the creases in sand dunes and helped distract me from the destruction that was internally tearing everyone in the room apart.

My father was surrounded by people who loved him. The Bracamontes family had not met me, except for a few of my closest relatives. I wanted to believe they were interested in me, but my heroin-addicted mother was, to them, a disease that was worse than what infected him. His family had strong roots in the Mexican and Mexican Indian Juaneño tribe community. My mother, Sicilian in ethnicity, acted like she was Mexican.

He was married before and had two kids—a boy and girl whom I never met but believe they were in his eerie hospital room as I weakly remember two teenagers crying together by the ceiling-mounted TV. It was on mute, but a Spanish soap opera was playing.

My father was behind a thick white curtain that radiated trepidation. The grating sound of metal on metal hurt my ears as the curtain rolled back like a 1920s horror film. Firm hands on my back guided me toward my father's bed, and my feet just slid along without me moving them in the slightest. Behind me, feminine murmurs were hushed, and I could feel every eye on me.

My dreamy mind clicked like the shutter button on a camera and captured ghastly images of my once invincible father layered in yellowish surgical tubes. They chaotically traveled in and out of the damp light green sheets and organically connected to the devices above his head, boasting red squiggly lines moving as slow as the tides of the ocean.

I could barely see above the edge of the bed where my head rested. There was a sense of urgency and a permeating degree of heated sadness. Shock waves of grief moved from the bottom of my feet to the top of my head, and I could feel my bottom lip protruding into a pout that encouraged unabashed tears.

I was so scared my body couldn't control its desperate tremors. I bravely placed my tiny hand on his once powerful arm. I played with the hair on his hand as I used to when he allowed me to ride in the front seat of his Mercury Cougar. His skin was clammy when I touched him, but there was still warmth there, and he made a soft sound in response. I heard hushed crying break the silence behind me. My eyes began to mist over, until tears separated themselves to fall onto his sheets, making tiny dark spots as evidence of my grief.

"Daddy?" My voice triggered another murmur and more whimpering behind me.

"Hi, Daddy," I said louder and continued to grip his arm, desperately clinging to his life. Despite the sounds of pain around me, I could not tear my eyes from the destruction that was my father.

His inflamed nose had an odd device corked deep within and made him gurgle while emitting small choking sounds that were painful to bear. Buried deeply into his throat was another hose. It was clear and looked to be angled in a way that made him recoil with every breath.

My dad's hair was mangled and matted to his forehead, except for a part that was shaved above the left ear. Dried-up maroon blood surrounded the wound and had seeped into the bandaging. A short tube was inserted into his head and, although not connected to anything, seemed important. My father was dying.

Angled slightly so that I could partially see his frail back through the crinkled, purplish-colored hospital robe, there was a fresh bandage in between his shoulder blades. It had a small dark red blood spot in the middle, and there was new bruising creeping outward. The soft-looking blanket was wrapped around his torso like a burrito, and it seemed he had a repetitive shiver coursing through his shockingly frail frame.

There was dreadful beeping echoing from the machines inside his room, and it created a monotonous environment. I could feel scalding hot tears pouring over my cheeks like a raging waterfall, and I had trouble breathing from a stuffed nose. My hand never left my father's arm. I could not bear to let him go because it had seemed if I left, that would be the last time I saw him.

It would be.

My mother brushed up behind me and wrapped her arms around me protectively, murmuring in my ear, "Everything is going to be okay, mijo." Even in that moment, I knew something was wrong with her beyond the grief. But it would not take long until more horrible events revealed what that was.

I remember saying to her through hyperventilated gasps, "I want to go home with you and Daddy." Tears were cascading down her cheeks, and all she could do was just nod and squeeze me tighter. I could only imagine how hard it was for her to even stand in that room while our world crumbled around us.

My body migrated to the plastic hospital chair next to his head, and I looked up into my father's hollow face. His handle-bar mustache was contorted, and his sunk-in eyes were bruised. My mother stood behind me, murmuring things in my ear, and I could sense she was near the breaking point. In that moment, she was about to become a single mom.

As I looked back into my father's face, I found him studying me with intense dark brown eyes. My eyes. My mother moved next to me, leaning on the bed and brushing the hair out of his face. She kissed him, and I could tell she wanted to ask him what to do but could not find the voice.

His huge hand was strong when it picked mine up, and he pulled me in close. I looked down to see the huge needle infusing my father with nutrients through a clear tube and almost cringed. Five-year-old me prayed for his pain to disappear so we could go home and escape this nightmare.

He put his hand on my wet cheek, rubbing off my tears. He always loved my hair, and I remember his face almost broke into sadness when he ran his fingers through my soft brown curls. There were tears in his eyes, which I had never seen before. The reality of those salty tears welling in his eyes scared me. I knew he was smiling through the terrifying realization that this was the last time he would be able to touch his young son. I think my presence put him at peace, and I instinctively knew he loved me very much.

"I love you, mijo," he hoarsely gasped around the tube in his throat.

"Love you too, Daddy," I said as bravely as I could muster.

He smiled his crooked smile and closed his deep-set brown

eyes. I never felt his rough hands on my head or heard my father's voice again. I don't remember leaving that hospital room, but I do recall being wrapped tightly around my crying mother as she walked toward her white Corolla in the parking lot and into a void that took no prisoners.

CHAPTER 2

BURIAL

Orange, California, 1986

━━━━━━━━━━━

The life of the dead is placed on the memories of the living.
—MARCUS TULLIUS CICERO

Foggy white mist encapsulated my vision. Though I knew the rolling images were not from a time past, I couldn't control the intensity of this memory, or its inevitable direction.

I was slowly walking without using my legs, gliding like a wraith, and following a dimly lit tunnel that resembled a subway. It was cold—bone-chilling cold—and I was not wearing shoes. The darkness weighed on my shoulders like a thousand mountains and pushed my feet into the earth.

I was in a church and had trouble seeing in to the lusterless cavern beyond. We walked down the middle of empty aisles, with dark wood pews surrounding me. Ghostly images moved in and out of my line of sight, blocking the amber light cascading from the stained glass windows.

My distraught mother had a negative aura hovering over her as she tried to guide me down the procession. Her presence in the church was not welcome, and the atmosphere crackled with profound tension. She was no saint, but a lost demon cast out.

I could not tell how many relatives and friends were sitting on the church benches, but it felt full. As my eyes sought the proverbial light at the end of this tunnel, a seizing pain began to penetrate my chest.

My father's family members were staring at me with pity and curiosity. They knew who I was but had never seen me before. I could sense they were saddened that my drug-addicted mother was the one taking care of me. They hated my mother and would never get over the power she held over my dad.

The forbidden love they shared evicted them from family. They came from two different worlds but found happiness in each other's companionship. There were many moments I would sneak around the corner of the kitchen to see them sitting together, smiling or laughing. A sweet happiness flowed around them in everything they did, from watching TV arm in arm to making dinner together in the small apartment.

I don't remember them being high around me or shooting up while I was near, but I was just a child who knew no wrong.

My body, on its own accord, made it to where a man in white robes stood, calmly observing my approach. His manner spoke of power and pain, but his humble eyes are what resonate.

A mahogany casket materialized before me, closed and dark. It frightened me to the point of shaking, and I knew my once strong father was inside. There were hushed murmurs all around me, and I was pushed on toward the dark embrace of that final moment.

I remember peering over my shoulder, and a sea of people was behind my mother. She was wearing black jeans and a mourning black blouse. There were so many faces looking back at me that when I tried to focus on one, they all blended chaotically. I could not see anyone; it was a hit to my equilibrium.

I am unsure if I touched my father's casket on that dark day. Buried in my grief, I could not manage to grasp what happened next. Everything felt wrong, and I sensed that my mother had completely lost control. What I couldn't have understood was that my father's side of the family would make no attempts to save me from the heroin-fueled volcano that my mother would become.

There was no transition to my mother's car from that ghostly church. Everything happened in the blink of an eye. We materialized in her car, and nothing else remained.

Beautiful Southern California hills dusted with wildflowers flowed by as we drove toward where my father was to be buried. I smelled a blend of desert sage, palm needles crushed on the ground, and pure white jasmine that reminded me of home.

We lived in a small one-bedroom place between Garden Grove and Orange that had big brown tiles on the roof. Many of the tiles were missing, and the others were worn down from the sun. The tan stucco walls were chipped and looked like they had not been painted since the first coat. There was an archaic black gate in the front that could have been the entrance to a Catholic cathedral.

The windows of my mother's white Corolla were halfway down, and from the back seat, warm air tickled my chin. She was solemn and silent, not even looking at me through the rearview mirror. I missed being seen, and I wondered if I ever would be again. My father would always look at me, keeping me in his sight.

He was looking at me like that on the day of the accident, and suddenly my battered mind took me back to that foreboding day.

•••

My dad wore a light blue button-down shirt that looked like a mechanic's uniform, and his thick black hair blew in the wind, making the back of his head look like a mop. His arm was resting comfortably halfway out of the car, holding a cigarette, and his dark brown-tinted glasses made him look like a gangster.

Thick white clouds made abstract pictures in the sky that swam quickly from one side of the sun to the other. I smelled the ever-present aroma of gasoline in the back of the car and the essence of grilled hamburgers from Carl's Jr.

My parents were whispering and smiling to each other in the front seat, yet my dad's brown eyes were constantly looking into the rearview mirror, checking on me. His mustache migrated smoothly toward his chin, ruffling slightly when he turned toward me, and caught the breeze just right. His hand would occasionally reach back and tickle my knee affectionately.

I belted out laughter, trying to get away from his playful attack.

Every time he glanced at me, there was either a quick wink or deep-set crinkles around his eyes from his crooked smile. I tried to reach out for him every few minutes, just to see if I could get him to look at me. He loved me so much, and his affection poured from him like water from a fountain. I could not control my excitement when I locked eyes with my dad. We had a special bond that nothing could break, or so I'd thought.

The wind pushed hard through the window as we made a sharp turn, back into reality. The memory softly faded.

My mother was going through the motions that kept her hidden safely within herself. Her unyielding grief seemed to spawn devilish horns that manifested after she had taken some drug in the church bathroom. I could always sense that spiral into intoxication from her drooping eyes, clenched silence, and lip-curling sneer that tarnished her beautiful face.

The manicured cemetery was anchored by mystical trees, and the wind was powerful that day. Giant pines and burly oaks glistened with morning dew. Jacaranda trees scattered around closer to the street, and their pale blue petals merged with the sky as if they were born together. Palm trees were skinny on the horizon and lent to the ocean feel of Southern California.

Those stewards of nature were majestic, standing guard over my father for eternity. The persistent wind blew untouchable to the world.

CHAPTER 3

JACARANDA

Fullerton, California, 1986

The oldest and strongest emotion of mankind is fear, and the oldest and strongest kind of fear is fear of the unknown.
—H. P. LOVECRAFT

The end of the first summer at home without my father, I lost the primary piece of my innocence.

My mother's soul sunk into a black-tar abyss, and her use of heroin filled what was left of a once beautiful heart. I retained sweet memories of when my father was alive. Lavender-scented bubble baths with them both laughing around the tub as I splashed. Big-wheeled scooters outside with my neighborhood friends conquering dark forces. Hunting sandy-white seashells and putting them on top of terribly molded sandcastles.

He was gone, and I wasn't dreaming.

● ● ●

Periwinkle-blue flowers fell ceremoniously from the twisted

jacaranda trees out front of my mother's latest boyfriend's house. Those petals created a hypnotic dance that swept me away from her betrayal. I was a curly-haired six-year-old boy, unable to comprehend the depth of devastation that was about to unfold.

My mother used to give me sweet-smelling baths, rubbing my tummy while holding me in the water. She'd tell me how much I looked like my father—how much my smile and ears reminded her of him. Those amazing moments of love were forgotten when she lost him to cancer as she found solace in the sickly sweet arms of heroin. My once soft-spoken mother had radiated kindness and love. In her place was an addict who used her body to find a place to hide with an older man named Bernie.

Those gentle times dwindled into self-loathing, as did her ability to even breathe a word about my father. She was lost for months or more to the numbing sorrow of loss. The shell of my mother journeyed into the heroine-induced chasm that left her passed out on the cold, green-tiled bathroom floor. She would silently set the lock, and I would lean weakly against that door, waiting for hours for her to emerge. She would wake from her fog, slow to remember she had a little boy. Mumbling through the echoing bathroom, she'd tell me to go to the kitchen to get the fresh strawberries she'd prepared earlier, softly coated in powdered sugar.

"Mijo, go to the kitchen— fresh strawberries and powdered sugar."

Bernie was a kind, older gentleman with white hair, likely in his late fifties. He was an engineer, with a beautiful blue Rambler on the corner of a well-established street in Fullerton. That home was the foundation for the loss of my childhood.

I am not sure if he knew how far gone my mom was, but he may have hoped he could be her savior.

There are painful triggers in my mind that bubble up from some sensory-driven reminder. Blurry images of my dad form in shadowy sequences and start with Christmas. He would be holding me in a bed in some bare apartment, laughing merrily through brown-tinted glasses. Other moments I would be sitting on his lap at the old glass dining table, and he never let me go.

Glimpses into what could have been hurt more than the desire for him to come back.

Bernie and the chromatic-blue home in Fullerton took over all the new memories that should have been with my dad. He was taken before I could know him, before he could see me grow into a loving son, and I felt so alone.

Bernie became my manipulative mother's meal ticket, as he kept us from a life on the streets of inner-city Orange County. I can recall when he would occasionally read Aesop's Fables to help me drift off to sleep. Bernie enjoyed oil painting in his front room that had shimmering green wallpaper, and he had a huge gun closet with an array of bullets along the inside wall near the bright white front door.

My mother and I shared the same pullout bed at night in the living room, even though there was another bedroom that Bernie had prepared for me, with a ceiling coated in shimmering blue paint. I remember being scared without her, though she was rarely around to comfort me. On many occasions, I found my mom in bed with Bernie, always with a look of shame on their faces.

"Your mom is sick, so I am taking care of her, Jeremy. Now, can you please knock before entering my bedroom?" Bernie would say in a flat, elderly tone.

My mother did what she had to for our survival, and there was an obvious history with Bernie. I was fortunate enough to have a roof over my head, food, and relative safety while we lived with Bernie. If only I'd known how brief it would be. He had an adult son named Mike, who would come by on occasion, and a daughter I had never seen but of whom he spoke fondly.

The jacaranda trees and their remarkable spring bloom released petals in a violet shower that slowly descended around the tree. Old gray sidewalks became a mess of crushed purples and released a unique smell that permeated the warm salt air. Beams of sunlight pushed through the flower canopy and crisped their fallen comrades on the ground.

Barefoot, I enjoyed scampering over the shaded parts of the sidewalk and feeling their chalky softness crush between my toes. I captured handfuls of the petals that fell from the beautiful trees above and made it rain sapphire perfection all around me as I flung them high into the heavens. My favorite cutoff army shorts would be coated in pollen and jacaranda petals.

My mother would get angry with me as I ran back into the house with my unwashed, purple crusty feet. She would tickle me when cutting my toenails, all while shaking her head and murmuring what a silly boy I was. Her soft, curly hair would fall across her perfect porcelain face, partially covering her sparkling brown eyes. When she looked up at me, I happily saw myself reflected in her.

These were the few moments before she got high.

She never hurt me physically, and although badly addicted to heroin, I knew she loved me deeply. The neglect that stemmed from her need for drugs humiliated her, but there was nothing that could stop the addiction, not even her small child. My mother took me with her on a few trips to acquire drugs, and I remember watching from the front seat.

I was scared the cops would show up any minute to take me away.

Like most attempts to get her hands on drugs, she slyly crawled through an unfamiliar first-floor window in a dirty apartment building. I felt the excruciating pain that radiated from her as she would hastily return to the car. Her embarrassment was palpable when she emerged from the house to find me looking at her.

"It's okay, mijo. I just forgot something at a friend's house," she would slur, getting in the car and driving away quickly.

These humiliating drug runs, with me in tow, were infrequent. Most of the time she left me alone in the house. Often this happened at least once a day. I was so terrified that I steadfastly stood by the front door, anxiously waiting for her white Corolla to turn the street corner.

Every light-colored car that appeared on our street got me excited enough to jump up with expectation. When I realized it was not slowing down, I slowly slumped along the paint-chipped door to the warped carpet. Sometimes it was an hour; other times it would seem to last all day. Bernie would often arrive home before my mom returned, upset to find I'd been left home alone again.

My mother never left our windows or doors open for more than a few minutes, the blinds always drawn. As I look back on those memories, the safe assumption was that she was under law enforcement surveillance for selling drugs, specifically heroin.

I could only imagine what she told Bernie when he would come home and find her strung out on the old sofa that had a creaky bed in it. I slept there many nights, too afraid to be in my lonely room. She was careful to hide her tools of the trade. The burnt and warped spoon looked like it was found after a house fire somewhere in the bathroom. I rarely saw the medical tubing wrapped around her arm, but sometimes she would forget to close the small door all the way.

Bubbling to the surface like the cooking of her heroin on that crispy spoon, I remember the snapping sound of a lighter flaming to life. Distant clicks from a well-used red Bic, I knew it was coming from the old bathroom to the left of the sofa couch. I could see a sliver of light from the dusty sconces on the well-worn carpet out front.

Moving slowly to not irritate the ancient springs of the couch, I rolled over the armrest like a ninja, knocking off the flower-patterned blanket. Low and crawling to the bathroom, my elbows collected dirt from the carpet. I smelled the tar before I saw the smoke bubbles on that gross spoon. My mother was leaning against the eighties-style bathtub in a pink T-shirt and jeans that had that elastic waist style.

Her long toes were painted a maroon color but chipped on the end, and that beautiful curly hair hid the paleness of her neck cascading around the tub edge. My mother's big brown eyes were not her own—droopy, lost within her poisoned mind, and downcast. She had already tied the fleshy tubing to her left arm and was preparing to fill a syringe with that deadly sauce. Once she flicked the end of the needle to remove bubbles from the ink-colored fluid, I could not watch anymore.

I quietly crawled backward toward the small box TV to continue watching *Teenage Mutant Ninja Turtles*, leaving the flower blanket on the floor. She would be in that drug chamber for hours and had already prepared my treat of strawberries with powdered sugar. Powdered sugar was what her lips would look like when she emerged on weak legs.

It was never enough. I just wanted her love, her smiling attention, and Mommy cuddles.

CHAPTER 4

RAID

Fullerton, 1986

Every form of addiction is bad, no matter whether the narcotic be alcohol, morphine, or idealism.
—CARL JUNG

The blue house was different the day I was taken. It felt open and alive, not closed off to the world.

A soft breeze kissed my cheek through the dusty screen door. Hazy blue tornadoes danced together out front, twisting over the petal-carpeted sidewalk, from a rarely open door. Birds were chatting outside, debating on whose jacaranda tree it was, and I felt no fear.

My neighborhood friends Aaron and Danny sat cross-legged next to me on the taupe carpet, watching my favorite movie, *Gotcha*. Their parents suspected I may have been homeschooled; I wasn't.

On that day, I felt happy and needed. My smiling mom was in the elevated dining room, frosting a chocolate cake and humming a song I wish I could remember. This was the same song she sang to help me drift to sleep at night as she played with my hair. I remember her long hair that day, falling about her shoulders. She seemed more aware, maybe only partially on drugs.

A few open pizza boxes were on the dining-room table, remnants of a lunch we had decimated earlier. Despite a full belly, it was hard to pull my eyes away from that chocolate cake and my beautiful mother. My friends had not seen *Gotcha*, and they were focused on the movie playing on the small TV. For some reason, I could not pay attention to the TV. I felt something wrong was in the air, but I could not have predicted what was about to happen.

The sound from the movie became a low muffle, and I could hear everyone's hoarse breathing.

Sharp boot steps replaced the sounds of harmonic birds, and a paralyzing silence followed. I heard the deep intake of my mother's breath behind me, and my little heart skipped a few beats. A forced breeze skimmed over my nose and smelled like my tree, with an imposing scent of cologne seemingly intruding on the wind. Bernie smelled like shaving cream, so I immediately knew this aroma didn't belong.

Innocent confusion was a prelude as a mild wind is to a gale.

Those tornadoes of precious blue perfection were kicked lifeless by dark shoes smeared with the jacaranda flower, shining wet with moisture. A black shadow invaded my limited line of sight to become a nightmarish sentinel taking up the entire doorway. Slowly, I looked up, feeling the anger radiating from the intense eyes of the one who, in rigid silence, was standing before me.

There was a pulsing vein in the middle of his forehead that

made him look like a fierce warrior, and although he knew I was
there, he never looked down at me. Instead, he was ruinously
glaring at my mom. As if out of a movie, the sparkling gold badge
on his belt caught my eye, and I glanced down to see his hand
resting on an onyx gun.

His badge took my mind back, and everything around disappeared into total recall.

●●●

Soft memories of a school I had rarely attended supplanted the
police officer in front of me. A quick thought back to a time barely
a year before, when I had met a kind cop. It was when I was first
taken from the elementary school I seldom attended.

A few months earlier, I was taken from school due to low atten-
dance and sent to a children's facility called Orangewood on the
grounds of parental neglect. The sickening smell that radiated from
that cruel place was overpowering. It was like the stench from a
gas station bathroom—dirty and alone.

The principal had no choice but to call the authorities, and it
must have been a tough day to be a teacher. Flashes of the fated
memory ignited, with teachers and school staff escorting me out
of the classroom, through a main entrance, and into the back of
a police car.

The first officer had been a young woman, who personally
escorted me to the Orangewood facility. I could sense the sadness
she was radiating. Arriving at the facility, the female officer hugged
me before handing me over to the staff. Orangewood, with its red-
brick fortress appearance, was born from the shattered dreams of

those who lost everything.

It was my first exposure to life in a group home. I had felt like I was being booked into a prison or psych ward, required to follow a checklist that consisted of boot camp–like precision. Isolated and unable to contain my overflowing tears, I clung to the hope that my mother or Bernie would rescue me soon.

The dark day at the house in Fullerton was a different experience but an all-too-familiar feeling. My focus popped back to reality.

They knew we were in the house; they knew exactly where everyone was and swooped in like eagles hunting mice. It was a tactical operation, and after coming out of my vivid memory of Orangewood, I could hear the distant crooning sirens from approaching backup.

My mom, whose eyes looked like teacup saucers, had a deathly pallid complexion. The sirens, paired with my mother's profound trepidation, sent glacial shivers down my arms. I gripped her hand tightly, but it was apparent she was prepared to bolt.

I watched her panicked gaze move quickly from the large man shadowed in the doorway to me, and then back again.

She screamed at the top of her lungs, "Run, mijo, run!"

It was a shrill sound that froze my tiny body and a paralysis that deafened even her painful cries. I remember noticing the jacaranda residue marking the carpet from the man's shiny boots as he drew his weapon on my mother.

Terrified, I tried to run toward the back door, but my little legs carried me about three feet before I was rolled up by another beast of a man who smelled of stale cigarettes. That scent reminded me of my mom, without the perfume cover-up and her car's air freshener.

My friends had quickly disappeared, thankfully escaping the terror that was unfolding. I never saw them again, and that was probably for the better.

"Hold still and stop screaming," the beast bellowed through clenched teeth, squeezing me tighter. When he yelled, spit erupted from his mouth like a hot geyser.

The gun was still pointed at her as the cop slowly moved in. She was not cooperating and would not listen to instructions.

"No, Mommy! Mommy, help me!" I screamed.

"Jeremy! Mijo! Don't hurt him, you assholes!" My mom cried, desperately moving closer.

The petal-crushing cop moved into a shooting position that froze her too.

My eyes never left my mother as the beast holding me back-pedaled out the house. The first man, with an angry vein pulsing from his forehead, tackled my uncooperative mother into the flower-patterned wall. Her chocolate-covered spatula went flying behind her and made a clanging noise that resonated in my ears.

The world mutated around our blue picture-perfect house, and every sound became a steady hum. Even the hypnotic movement of the iconic jacaranda seemed to pause. Police sirens became a deafening whisper, nosy neighbors moved in slow motion while their shaking bobbleheads continued to bounce around, and my mom's sizzling tears were all that I could see, all that I could concentrate on. She was in pain, and I couldn't save her.

"Don't hurt my mommy! Don't hurt my mommy!" I screamed

in that child-pitched voice. The beast continued to trudge toward
a black sedan that had no markings.

Confused and crying, I whimpered desperately for my mom.
She had finally been caught. She was handcuffed and dragged out
of the house like the people I had seen in movies. Face down in the
dirty grass, crushed jacaranda petals weaved through her long hair
and caked onto her beautifully flushed cheeks. She was staring at
me through bloodshot eyes, emanating anguish, when I saw her
suddenly stop struggling. In that moment, I realized for the first
time I would never feel her comforting arms around me again.

"Jeremy, mijo, it's okay. Don't worry. I will see you soon and
come get you—I promise, I promise." There was more muffled
screaming as the cops dragged her to the patrol car.

My mother appeared to be a limp rag doll tossed into the back
of a nondescript windowless white police van, and I was completely emptied of warm, saltwater tears. I was so angry in that
moment my tears returned with vengeance. There would be no
more smiles from me, especially after the beast placed me into the
back of his isolated squad car.

"Son, please be a good boy. We are waiting for a social worker
to come to talk to you and take you somewhere you can't be hurt
anymore," he grunted, avoiding eye contact.

I desperately needed my mother, and I told him that. I begged
him to help me save her. I remember the etched sadness on his face
as he said, "Sorry, son, your mother is in big trouble."

His relief was apparent when an older, red-haired woman from
child protective services ushered me into another vehicle.

"Hey, Jeremy, things are going to be scary, but I will be with you, okay?" she stated.

The white police van where my mother was held captive had an escort of a half dozen squad cars with their intense flashing lights bouncing off everything reflective—windows, stop signs, and cars—but there was no sound. It was silent, and only my labored breathing felt loud.

The concerned neighbors instantly came out of their homes and operated like they knew this event would happen. I was sure it was one of them who had likely seen my tear-streaked face plastered to the glass door during school hours and had enough of my negligent mother leaving me home alone. The fact that she was an alcoholic, chain-smoker, and a junkie was just a bonus.

I was just a baby. I only needed love. Yet that was the last day I ever touched my mother. It was the last day I smelled her warmth. That day changed everything, and the heartbreaking reality was that I would never feel her embrace again.

● ● ●

Staring out the moving vehicle while my favorite indigo trees faded behind me, I could only imagine when I would swing through their soft embrace again.

Everything was a vividly colorful blur as we rode along through the cityscape of Orange County, and I felt an explosion of hostility inside my already beaten soul. There was only one place that would take me in now.

My crying had collapsed into miserable silence, and I began to remember all the disturbing times my mom made me hide under the bed when someone—be it police or not—would knock on the door. The hours of quiet hiding in closets or bathrooms when she thought she saw shadow figures outside a shaded window. She was not protecting me; she was evading capture.

"How are you doing back there, kiddo?" asked the sweet-smelling lady with eyes like warm molasses. There was a baby seat in the back of her jade-colored sedan, and it smelled like popcorn.

I intentionally ignored her and looked out the window, toward the dwindling amber sunset, in hopes this horrible nightmare could be blinked away.

"Everything is going to be okay. The place we are going to will take good care of you," she said as she nervously chewed on her lip.

"Where are we going?" I asked. "I want to go back home," I said, betraying my previous vow of silence.

"It's called Orangewood, Jeremy," she said in a low tone.

I knew where I was going, but she didn't know I knew.

Her monotone words dulled to nothingness in the car as my thoughts slid back into the black oblivion of the last time I was taken. What a terrible place.

The sleeping area smelled like the hospital room my father lay in before he died. Many living spaces reeked of old, rotting clothing from a vintage retail shop. It was a hollow place, where a small, scared child lived in constant fear of being abused by other kids. These bullies were taken from their families not because their parents did something wrong but because the child was downright evil.

It felt like eternal confinement, where freedom consisted of walking outside with walls of barbed wire and residing next to a juvenile hall. One could see the troubled kids in their jumpsuits across the double fence to the left of Orangewood.

Time warped as the social worker slowly drove up to the haunted hotel-style roundabout entrance. Dusk took over the purpling sky as the night seemed to be approaching too fast. Moonlight appeared behind the bright floodlights encompassing the entire property and formed a haze around the large metal ingress doors painted beige.

A stoic security guard was waiting outside with a clipboard and grim look. His dark blue pants were wrinkled, and he held a flashlight that seemed like it would attract all the wayward children like moths to a flame. Compassion was left in the car seat next to me, and I was pushed forward toward the rest of the end of my life.

Shuffling back into the terrifying orphanage made my little body shake uncontrollably, and I helplessly looked around at the blurred emotionless sentries who were now in charge of my very existence. My wounded heart knew my mother was not coming back this time to save me, and the true terror of being all alone came when I jumped in fear from the metal door mercilessly slamming closed behind me.

The social worker mysteriously vanished, and I could not blame her. It was emotionally horrible for them to put puppies into the kill shelter.

The bright white hallway ahead of me was painfully familiar and led into a living dungeon that no six-year-old boy should ever have to behold. I looked around one last time for a hidden savior, before I was escorted toward a world of complete isolation. I could not fathom what was going to happen next.

Happy Easter, SON

MY DEAR JEREMY,
It seems like only yesterday
that you were little, Son,
Enjoying all the
Easter treats
and making Easter fun,
And though,
as years have come and gone,
you've outgrown
childhood things,
You never will outgrow the love
this "Happy Easter" brings!

I LOVE YOU
with ALL MY
HEART.

MOM

CHAPTER 5

NIGHTMARES

Orange, California, 1986–1987

---

*Let us put our minds together and see what life we can
make for our children.*
—SITTING BULL

Like a monstrous black hole loomed the imposing closet of Plato. It held all the bed linens and clothing rationed out to the array of estranged children at Orangewood. Most were donations, smelled musty, and did not fit well. They were clean enough.

The closet was claustrophobically narrow and appeared to rise ten feet. It boasted beige floor-to-ceiling cabinets on each side, completely packed with a variety of children's clothing. In the back, there were piles of donated items flowing out of black garbage bags, not yet sorted. The clothing insulated the space, making it uncomfortably warm.

Worn shoes ranging from boots to sandals were in the cubbies along the bottom, stored by size. Some clothing was held for special occasions in the church section near the trash bags of clothing.

I was the only child around this late in the evening, and the tawny lighting was dimmed low, creating a forlorn ambiance. Distantly, I could hear talking, but the direction was misplaced due to the auditorium-like ceiling. Lethargic fern plants were staged along the corners of the area and took on the droopy nature of Orangewood.

"Where is everyone?" I squeaked too loudly. Silence threatened.

The mundane staff member who processed me in said in a monotone voice, "Everyone is getting ready for bed." He was silent and seemed indifferent, like he had done this before. We waited patiently in front of the clothes closet for someone with a key.

I had been questioned about my name, birth date, and information on why I was there. This led to my mother's arrest, and I cried talking about it. Even with the forced silence, I knew the staff member cared, as he stayed close to me. He unconsciously reached out, patting my shoulder.

"It's a bit late, buddy. We are working to get you a room to sleep in," he said.

The night shift must have not been expecting any kids. Another staff member walked up to the big closet, and she radiated kindness. "Hey there, cutie pie," she said.

Her happiness made me hint at a smile, and that was enough for her as she opened the closet. She picked out what looked to be comfy yellow flannel pants and a light blue T-shirt before ruffling my hair.

I remember bleach-smelling showers and a small window to a white room that had a very heavy metal door. We were monitored during those showers, and it was timed.

Two small beds could be seen in the darkness of the room they chose for me. "Go ahead and put your stuff on the empty bunk, then head back out," my warden said.

Sensing another person in the room, I ran out quickly after throwing my stuff on the bunk. There was a pile of folded linens and a pillow at the end of the bed. I heard the door make a sound like air getting sucked out of a vacuum upon closing. Who was this kid? Hopefully not a bully.

I was guided back to the community space, and it smelled like chicken noodle soup. I was hungry. Mr. Silent had offered me a bag of cookies earlier, which I gobbled up, and a small carton of milk.

After so many painful experiences, seeing poor little children taken from their families, I am sure it took a toll on the staff at Orangewood.

Behind me, I heard laughter, and when I turned around, a flamboyant African American lady with colorful nails was swiftly approaching us. She seemed to understand that I was frightened because she came right up and knelt to hug me. Her long nails patted my head, and I immediately began to cry.

Tears poured down my face, and she whispered, "It's okay, baby. It's okay."

Why was this happening to me? I cringed inwardly, wondering if all the other kids got taken from their mothers.

A dark and dangerous hallway opened before me, and I passed a guard station that was enclosed in glass. It was situated to see at all angles. There was a soft rose-colored glow that reflected off the glass. I had to squint to see in but could not make out if there was a staff member sitting inside.

Looking behind me, I felt terror grasp at my soul, and the confusion in my mind was only getting worse. I missed my mom, even Bernie. I held on to a childlike hope they would save me from this shadowy world that had pulled me into its icy embrace.

Nail lady let me use the bathroom, and I began to cry silently walking in alone.

Nothing had changed since the last time my feet felt the cold embrace of the white tiled floors and the sickly smell that flowed out. Water saturated the floor from a leaking shower, and mildew overpowered the bleach.

This was my second time here, but I knew it would not be my last. It couldn't be, if heroin was the oozing kryptonite of my mom's world. She had an alcoholic sister who was not going to help, and my father's side of the family had no idea where I was.

Time to fend for myself in a world that offered little forgiveness and enjoyed exploiting weakness. There was nothing to grasp on to for support, nothing to hold on to for buoyancy, and it was painfully obvious this was going to be routine for a long time.

The hallway was dark and silent, like a hospital late at night. Nail lady, who took over for Mr. Silent, stopped in front of my white steel door with its small, barred window embedded toward the top. Each room looked like a vault, and the fear pulsated under each door.

Tears welled up in my eyes again, and she gave me a quick hug while holding the door to the shadowy room. She pulled out a flashlight and aimed it toward the floor. It was the same tile as everywhere else. I could see the two military-style metal-spring beds, a small nightstand in the middle, and two dressers.

The other child was asleep in the opposite bed but started to stir. Nail lady helped make the bed quickly, which I had never done before. I remember having trouble getting the pillowcase on and her laughter when I smacked myself.

As she walked out of the room, she looked back with a sad smile on her face that reminded me of the CPS officer who brought me here and whispered, "See you tomorrow, baby."

The door closed with a soft, methodic click. It was a child's prison.

● ● ●

Dazzling fluorescent lights erupted within my eyelids, causing me to blearily wake up from a horrific landscape that left me shaking. I was taken from my mother and deposited back at Orangewood. Reaching out for my mom, I instead smacked my hand into a wall, almost jamming my finger.

Adjusting to my surroundings and trying to blink away a pulsating red haze of angry stars, I realized it wasn't just a bad dream. I was back in a disruptive reality, where I had no choice but to robotically adjust to what the master says. I was in the white room with my new roommate, who had already made his bed and was gesturing for me to get up. He looked to be a couple of years older than me and big.

"Hurry up. Don't get me in trouble, or I will kick your ass," he said, turning away from me.

The sheets smelled like burnt plastic and sanitizer. The blanket was scratchy brown wool and stiff. The bed creaked from old metal springs, and I lost my balance as it leaned toward the floor with my weight. The other kid laughed.

There was a soft grating sound coming from outside the steel door facing us, and I realized it was the release of a lock. I heard our door being opened from the outside, not realizing we were locked in, and a male staff member poked his head through.

"Hurry and make your beds, then stand outside your door," he said to no one in particular.

The other kid, whose name I can't remember, looked at me in confusion. I had not even started making the bed. I wondered what the hurry was but tried to throw the blanket over my pillow as best as I could. My mother had always made the bed, and the way I did it looked messy.

I was in the toddler ward during my last visit, and that was in another building nearby. There were no locks on the doors, and it had a different atmosphere. I was now in the preteen ward, and it radiated violence.

I was the last one done, and that was a mistake.

Everyone stared at me with menace, and I felt completely alone. The new fish.

We were in the bright hallway, which had twenty rooms on each side or more. It was eerily silent, except for the occasional whisper or foot shuffle. There was a wide variety of children, all of whom looked miserable or mean. We formed a single-file line for our daily gift of clothes, and my cell was near the front.

A few of the older kids down the hall were staring at me and making evil faces. Their body language spoke of anger, and they saw fresh meat to dice up. These terrible kids were the bull sharks in a pond full of minnows, and the ones who I knew would be hard to evade.

Shuffling toward the big closet in socks that were too big, they took roll call, and my name came up. I heard someone behind me snicker and make fun of my last name. It was hard to pronounce and an easy target.

Chaotic is a gentle term for the ridiculous pandemonium that embodied handing out clothes. The older kids pushed ahead at the last minute, trying to find the coolest-looking clothes. They snatched the jeans that had designs on them. As they passed by me, I was slammed against the wall repeatedly until my body crumpled from the pain. They cussed at me and laughed at me as I tried to crawl away from their abuse.

I stood up slowly after the first wave of deviants, but a second wave came next. I hit the wall, and my body crumpled to the ground. I tried my best to get up quickly without crying, but it didn't work. I went from the front of the line to the back before I realized what was happening.

I got yellow shoes, and that was just fine.

After the clothes drama panned out, we formed another line toward our rooms. The kids were loud and energetic, some screaming and others pushing simply because they could. I noticed a few other kids, a bit younger than the first, looking at me in a way that made me shiver. Everyone knew who the fresh meat was.

I got safely back to the room and changed quickly. It was time to go to breakfast. My roommate seemed uncaring and was already out the door before I had gotten my shirt on. The doors were unlocked, which could mean trouble later.

Everything was moving so fast I did not have time to be scared, and that innocent bliss I previously lived in began to unfold into a frenzied assembly of lone survival.

I was six going on seven and looked five. We lined up in the main common area to head toward breakfast. This time I kept up in my yellow shoes.

The dining facility was disorganized and a scary place. It was as big as a high school basketball court and full of green round tables with matching foldable chairs. Kids hollered and complained about the taste of the food. Fruit, bread, and other items were scattered or squashed all over the shiny linoleum flooring.

The place was lit up like a Friday-night football game. I smelled chicken noodle mixed with a hint of syrup. The saltiness in the air made my mouth water, and I again found myself pushed to the back of the line. The biggest kids were at the front, and the staff members looked resigned while some were just shaking their heads. They stood around the parameter in pairs.

Our ragtag group was directed to an area close to the kitchen turnstile, and I was introduced to powdered eggs. I still remember spitting them back out on my plate and gagging while the other kids laughed at me.

The bad breakfast at Orangewood made me think of eating at Norms with my dad. Made me think of good food and his love. I missed him so much. If he were alive, he would have never let this happen.

Most of the other children did not even get eggs, but waffles and bacon.

After the imperial breakfast, we had recess in the middle of the facility. Multiple French doors led to the play area from the dining facility. Some kids were already walking out—mostly the older, savvier ones. The faster we ate, the longer we played.

We had to eat most of our food, or we could not be excused, and the angry spit-out eggs were staring up at me, knowing I would be one of the last to leave.

Orangewood had a large common area surrounded by other brick buildings, like that of the preteen ward, and laid out like the Pentagon. The trees, sporadically placed within red-brick planters, were typical Southern California spruces but small and smelled of eucalyptus. Kids were sitting around them in groups. Others were running around, probably staying clear of the bullies.

Trying not to cry, I carefully walked out of the cafeteria with my head down, hoping someone would see me. My eyes darted everywhere, looking for bullies. Day one, day ten, day fifty, every day blurred together. I was fearful, and I was scared to death.

In the far corner, a dramatically constructed church rose high and next to the teen ward. One for the boys and one for girls. The girls' preteen ward was next to ours but before the infant area. There was a location at Orangewood dedicated to small infants and children as well. The sense of loss and loneliness overpowered everything that existed in my lost soul.

I was not prepared for the pushing and shoving when leaving breakfast. I was small for my age and was immediately knocked over past the first set of trees, out of sight from the staff members. At first I thought it was an accident, but when I looked up, there were a bunch of young boys around me, glaring down in a frightening way.

I tried to get up, but someone kicked my arms out from underneath me.

I felt sand thrown in my face, laughter from all around, and then the kicking started. I had never felt pain like that or pressure that sucked the air out of my lungs. It forced me to gasp for breath, like a fish out of water.

"You look like a girl. Are you a girl?" I heard someone snicker.

"What a bitch." Another laughed.

The tears came before I could stop them. I felt hands grab my ankles, pulling me over the cement. My head bounced over something hard, and it was tough to breathe. More laughter shamed me into screaming for help, and I was so scared I kept my eyes squeezed closed.

"Help! Help!" I pleaded.

Before I realized what had happened, it was over. When I finally pried my eyes back open, there was nobody around me, and I was lying underneath jade-colored monkey bars. Sand filled my ears and was caked in my hair, all the way down to the scalp. I felt it down my pants and in my underwear. I shivered uncontrollably and tasted blood.

I got up slowly. I got up and pretended nothing happened.

My elbows were bleeding from long red scratches that looked like burns, and my fingernails looked like the tips were run through with a shredder. My pants had the start of new holes in them, and I wondered if this was going to happen every day. Tears came in a wave of wheezing anger I could not control.

I looked around and realized all the kids were running back toward their wards. If I didn't move fast, I was going to be late.

I tried to run back but felt a sharp pain in my side, so I hobbled back instead. My shoes had been taken, so I continued in my dirty socks.

The nice lady with the nails opened the double doors to the preteen ward, and I held back to hide. She had a clipboard in her hand and was preparing to do a routine check to make sure all the kids were accounted for when she noticed the condition I was in.

She didn't say much other than, "Oh, you poor boy."

I immediately attached myself to her leg, hoping she would stop the embarrassment.

She took me to the infirmary, and an older nurse who smelled like cinnamon rolls bandaged me up. They both walked me back to the preteen ward, where all the kids were lounging. It was a mistake to be seen with them.

Tons of kids were sitting or playing on the pleather couches, chairs, and gathered on the rugs that covered the tiled floor. They were talking or yelling at each other in an elementary school–type setting. Eyes shifted to me, and a quiet filled the room, with all attention pointed at me.

The nurse said, "Find a place to sit, buddy."

A huge rolling board with colored stars was the focus of attention, and a staff member was calling out names, then placing a star next to the designated spot. It was time for the leveling system.

Gold was the best, red was the worst, and other colors came between, like green, blue, or yellow. There were a lot of red stars on that board.

I was an animal in a cage, and everyone was looking to see what trick I would do. I plopped onto one of the chartreuse-colored couches, trying to become invisible. My feet did not touch the ground, and my shoes made squeaky sounds over the plastic shell.

"It's okay, Jeremy. Nobody is going to hurt you here," said the lady with the clipboard.

I was not so sure.

"Your name is now on the level system over there, but you won't get your first star until tomorrow. Be a good boy," she concluded.

Watching her walk away, my eyes misted over again. I was covering my face so no one would see. The boy next to me looked to be around nine or ten and was staring at my elbow with a grin on his face. No friends there.

The staff member in front of the level system was still calling out names and putting up stars when an older man came over to kneel in front of me. He introduced himself as the director and wanted to speak to me about what happened during the recess.

He took me to his office, which had a huge USC rug in the middle, and gave me a piece of chocolate to reassure my unsure attitude. "Jeremy, I understand you got hurt at recess today. What happened?"

Telling him about what happened made me wonder how many other kids got this treatment on their first day and if he could make a difference. He told me that they would make sure this did not happen to me again and patted my head. He ushered me back to the play area, which was right outside his office.

That was that, I guessed, but there was no way it was over.

Months went by. I got beat up many more times and had two different roommates. The second smelled of dirty feet. The food got increasingly worse, or so I thought. I began to hate vegetables, which dissolved together in an amazing display of half-frozen green mush.

I learned from the veteran kids around me that if I threw a bit of the salad or other vegetables on the ground and smoothed food over my plate, it looked like I tried to eat.

Sundays were for church at Orangewood. It was tough listening to the lethargic drone of the monotone pastor's sermon with someone constantly flicking my ear. I dreaded that compact place of worship and how it became a boiling pot of dank bodies meshed in one perfect, chaotic assembly.

Claustrophobic insanity paired with children and young, severely neglected teens sadly never created an attentive audience. Even in a church, I got smacked around.

Recess was a daily reminder that I was living in an institution that caged its dwellers from the outside in. The perimeter had a high chain-link fence boasting devilish barbed wire that was as foreboding as it was striking. The rumor was that it electrocuted anyone who touched it, and even untrue, I believed it.

It's distressing the appalling things a child can pick up in an orphanage. It adds to the true loss of untouchable innocence, and once stolen, it was gone forever. Many of the children at Orangewood were not removed from their homes like I was. They were placed there because of the torment they put their poor families through. Those were the tainted souls who demonstrated evil traits and the ones to watch out for.

Early one morning, when the air was thick with the salt from the sea, I was outside at recess close to the bike racks that were attached to the preteen ward. I was called over by the nail lady, who seemed more jovial than usual. "Jeremy!"

"Jeremy, there is someone here who is going to be your guardian until we can find a more permanent place for you."

I did not know what a guardian was, but if it got me out of Orangewood, I was in.

She guided me over toward the security station near the big clothes closet and some tables that resembled large barstools. A heavyset woman was standing there, looking a little out of place but radiated a gentle nature. I remember her in purple.

"Jeremy, this is Donna. You will be living with her and her two children."

"Hi, Jeremy," Donna said sweetly.

"Hello," I said shyly. My stomach was hurting, and I felt nervous.

I wondered where my mother was and if she was in jail. She was not trying to get me back if I was moving to another home. Was she okay? Was I going to see her again?

Donna was a foster mother who occasionally let her house become an immediate shelter home (ISH) for children needing help. I was one of those neglected kids. She looked down at me with a large, warm smile and knelt, saying, "Let's get you out of here."

We walked through those doors the opposite way, with the fire-red bricks behind me, and it felt great. I had a foreboding feeling though. This was not the last time a dungeon would lock me up again, but I pushed that aside.

JEREMY,

Hi baby, do you
mind if I still
call you that? you'll
always be my baby
boy.

I love you with
all my heart. I
can't explain why I
messed up so bad all I can tell you,
& I mean this, never did a day & does
a day goes by that I don't think of
you.& my heart, hurts that I let you
down so badly. Will you ever forgive
me. I'm going to be gone I think for
a long time but I'll always love
you. auntie Sherry is still trying
to have you over to her house. She &
I talk about how good your doing.
I'm so very proud of you, your voice
sounds so grown up. I must tell
you once again how proud mommy
is of you. Your a little man now. I
realize things have been really hard
for you but baby I truly love you
with all my heart & soul.

Bernie is trying to get it worked
out that he can talk with you. He
loves you & always will.

Drugs have ruined so much of my

life and in turn have hurt you and kept us apart. Jeremy, drug addiction is a terrible thing.

Tell me what kind of things do you like to do now. I'm glad the new people that take care of you are so nice. They seemed very nice, I talked to the lady for a little while on the phone. I just can't tell you enough how very sorry I am for all the pain I've caused you.

Have you had a nice summer? what is your favorite subject at school?

Jeremy send me some pictures please. I have a bulletin board in my room & that way I can show all my friends what a beautiful (HANDSOME) son I have. That way I can look at you every day & feel a little closer to you.

I love you now, always and forever...

Love,
Mommy

CHAPTER 6

SHELTER

Westminster, California, Spring 1987

Our houses are such unwieldy property that we are often imprisoned rather than housed in them.
—HENRY DAVID THOREAU

The sensation of loss was far worse than the feeling of being lost. I was hidden within the forgotten shadows of Orangewood until that day.

I felt alive as Donna drove me away in her car. She hugged me and protected me all the way to that vehicle. She put my seat belt on for me, patted my head, and squeezed my shoulder before getting in herself. Her every thought was focused on helping children, and I felt it pouring from her.

The first night in her home, the nightmares started. It would eventually lead to my undoing in that gentle home.

A gray dirt path curved out before me, and the heels of my feet had made long, dragging lines toward where I was dropped or maybe thrown. I was back at Orangewood, possibly, and could see the church in the distance but nothing else. My face was covered in scratches from sand and pebbles, though I was unsure how they got there. Someone had stolen my shoes, and I felt blood dripping down from my elbows.

Standing up, the darkness closed in with soft pressure, and I could not escape it. On each side of the path, the blackness was so profound I felt as if I was walking in space. Behind me, the path began to disappear and forced me to quicken my step, quicken my heartbeat.

I could feel hot tears fly away into space beyond, and the wet mercury opals became distant stars watching my capture. The church was farther away than when I started, and space had stolen the path ahead of me. There was nowhere else to run, and the end of the line loomed before me. The evil taunted me and was about to encase me, when it retracted suddenly, almost painfully.

From somewhere far away, I heard kindness. "Jeremy, honey, did you have another nightmare?" Donna asked.

Morning sunlight filtered through thin curtains, creating a soft radiance around Donna's gentle face, like a halo. She was an angel who saved me from the brick pits of Hades. She pulled the covers back so that I could cool down and rubbed my damp hair, calming my fear.

I nodded my head groggily and mumbled something about Orangewood. This was not the first time I woke up scared in her home from a dream that would not end. On numerous nights, I woke up in fear from that place. Reliving the night I was taken from my mother made going to bed an anxious time.

I started having stomach problems. It humiliated me, and I could not figure out how to fix it. This stemmed from my mother shooting up inside the subway-green bathroom we shared back in Fullerton to ger her heroin fix and my heart pumping fear of it thereafter. How could one go to the bathroom when it was over-taken by a junkie?

What was a small, candle-size flame of apprehension turned into a blaze of dread when it came to using the perilous bathroom. At Orangewood, menace waited in or around the restroom. A sneaky kid would pee on my feet in the stall or throw wet toilet paper on me or worse. This was true trauma.

My knotted stomach would turn in on itself, and to me there was nothing more frightening than sitting alone on the toilet. It was a constant reminder of my mother's heroin addiction and the rocket-launching of my life without a life in an institution.

It got to the point where I was so scared to go to the bathroom it would show in my underwear. Donna was understanding but did not know how to fix this problem, which I think would ulti-mately end in my return to Orangewood. I was just too young to understand the implications of my pain or my trauma.

Donna's presence as a mom made me want to hug her, and she never seemed angry. She lived in a quaint single-story home in Westminster, from what I remember, but it could have been another city close by. It was nestled around large pines that pro-vided constant shade. Her cottage home was a natural sanctuary protecting the innocent from harm.

There were other kids there as well, two of whom were hers and one other foster. The foster boy named John was protective of me and made sure I was okay. He taught me multiplication, and I remember him saying over and over, "Ten times ten equals one hundred." Looking back, he repeated almost everything he said.

The other kids accepted me immediately, but I think it was because they knew I was only there for a short period. I was much younger than them, and it created a divide. The longer I stayed with Donna and her beautiful family, the harder I thought of myself anywhere else. I missed my mother terribly, but living in that cottage pushed the pain down somewhere hidden.

While at Orangewood, I did not have a single visitor. It was depressing. Feathers of jealousy were the crown I wore on my head when the other kids played happily with those who loved them. It was not lost on the bullies, who knew I had no one.

They would point at me or make faces when their families were not paying attention, mouthing things silently, like, "No one loves you," or "You're an orphan."

Donna and my social worker contacted Aunt Sherri on my mother's side, her only sister and also a negligent mother in her own right. She was an addict, but that poison was copious amounts of alcohol mixed with pot.

My social worker, Michael, had short brown hair, cut in a flattop, and came to visit me once a month while at the shelter home. He seemed genuinely concerned for my well-being and asked me repeatedly, "You sure you are okay, buddy? Anything you need to tell me?"

I believe that stemmed from Donna's constant fear of my stomach issues, and it was embarrassing.

My aunt lived off welfare in a low-income apartment deep within the ghetto of Anaheim. I got pink eye from the community pool there one time as a little child before my dad died.

She had a sandy-haired son, who was slightly younger than me, named Andrew. He was a good-natured cousin who loved Disney characters, especially Goofy. When my mother and her sister would visit each other, Andrew never let me out of his sight, and I was okay with that.

Sherri and Bernie once came to see me at the shelter home on a warm day in Southern California. It was the first time I saw anyone from before I was taken. Across from each other in the small living room, the air cackled with awkwardness.

I don't remember the conversations we had, but I am sure it had to do with getting me reunited with my mom—they knew that would not happen. They only came that one time, and it was the last time I ever saw my friend Bernie. His parting gift was a shiny new calculator watch and a sad smile.

After that visit in the shelter home from Aunt Sherri and Bernie, time moved slow like the sand in an hourglass. Things shifted toward an end I knew was coming. I could tell from the way Donna treated me that something was afoot.

●●●

There was a picnic-style table in the dining room connected to the kitchen where all the kids ate, which had a beeswax polish on it. At that table, I was introduced to the sloppy joe, and it will forever be my first thought eating that sandwich. Dinner aromas overpowered the sawdust smell of the home, and everything felt warm.

While living at Donna's, I was not on a behavioral system that consisted of charts with colored stars, but we all wanted to please her. I don't remember any of the kids doing anything bad or getting in trouble. The fear of being taken away was a daily dose of reality for institutionalized kids. Donna had an infectious kindness, and she gave all the children in her home as much love as her heart could pump.

She knew I had trouble learning due to my mother's neglect and strived to help me get caught up in school, but it was not an easy battle. Along with my stomach issues, depression, and horrific nightmares, I was a child who took a lot of her time. Too much of her time.

The public school I attended was not like the paste-induced mob at Orangewood, where learning consisted of trying to dodge spitballs from the older kids. I had never been a part of a kindergarten class, and the experience was disheartening. I remember sitting around other kids who knew how to do some form of reading and arithmetic. I feared the public bathrooms and other kids making fun of me.

I was allowed to walk home with the other foster kids after school because it was so close. Sometimes we even stayed late to play games with other normal children. These are the things most kids take advantage of.

Since I was a ward of the court, I qualified for school lunch, and I was the only light-skinned kid in line. This caused a lot of bullying. No one believed I was Hispanic in any way.

One day, during lunch, I was waiting to enter the cafeteria, when someone kicked the bottom of my shoe while I shuffled forward. He kicked me so hard I fell forward on my knees, and then he pushed me by the back of my head into a metal fence that formed the line. He was a Mexican kid and had a big group of friends pointing and laughing at me. He called me *güero*, which meant "white boy," and pushed me out of the line.

"You don't belong here, bitch." He laughed. His friends laughed, too, and all of them flipped me off as I lay on the ground.

There was dirt on my clothes, my shoes were scuffed, and everyone was staring. It was hard to get back up, but I did. Back in line, at the very end, way behind that mean group.

I never told Donna, nor did I stop getting my lunch. It did not happen every day, but the bullying was more than enough to make me cry. It got to the point where I would only eat my lunch with John, who was older, and when he was there, nobody pushed me around.

John was my roommate at Donna's house, and he was nice to me. He seemed to not care about my issues and showed me how to use all sorts of home-improvement tools. We became good friends, and for the first time I began to feel what it was like to have a brother.

Camping with her family was my most vivid memory, and Donna made it a mystical experience. She had an old white RV we all played around in on our drive up to Big Bear Mountain a couple of hours away. When we got to the campsite, she seemed to know everyone there, and I immediately felt right at home.

Nights of burnt s'mores, amazing bonfires with family, happy dogs running around, and the smell of fresh pine trees will forever be with me.

John and I would stay in the tent behind the RV, while the other kids slept inside. One night we were in the tent, and an animal was making mysterious noises just outside the entrance. We thought it was a bear, but it was most likely a raccoon. John, as the older one, tried to be brave, but we could not control our shaking sleeping bags.

In the morning, we told Donna about the "bear" and elaborated on our bravery. John let me borrow his Magic Johnson Lakers jersey, which looked like a yellow dress on me, but I did not care. I followed him everywhere, and I think he liked the company. We would sit around the campfire before anyone else got there and talk about our favorite G.I. Joes. Mine was Snake Eyes, the first action figure my mother bought me.

Those piping-hot s'mores, nicely burnt hot dogs, and great times in front of a campfire created a place in my heart that is still here today. I was never able to make the s'mores back then without breaking the graham cracker, so Donna would let me burn the marshmallow while she made the rest.

During those happy times, I never thought about what my mother did. The nightmares became less of an issue, and I did my best to do the right things.

●●●

Late one day after school, months after that camping trip, the news came.

Fate's angry fingers slithered back into my life and snatched me from my fantasyland. My social worker, Mike, was waiting for me on the couch with an intense look in his eyes. I knew something was not right when he dropped his eyes in sadness. I knew it was bad.

After some small talk, he said, "Jeremy, we must take you to a group home. I am so sorry. It is a good home not far from here called Child Help."

A punch to the gut would have been better. A punch to the face would have been more welcome. "Why do I have to leave? Please don't make me go," I whispered.

Mike had no answer and made his way to the front door.

I begged Donna to stay as she held me tight. She was crying softly and rubbing my hair like she did when I had nightmares.

Just another kid with no family. A lost boy who had issues too difficult to deal with.

Mike was not charming this time but sad. His eyes hurt, and I could tell he cared about me. I did not understand what I had done. I did not know what was going on. I was only six and blamed myself.

As I packed up my things, clothes, and toys Donna had given me, I began to cry hysterically. Why could I not just be accepted and loved and given a chance?

Donna was crying softly again, saying she would try to help get me back, but I knew from the tragic look on her face that was a hollow promise. Mike was waiting grimly outside for me by his car. I was sure this part of the job created the wrinkles on his forehead.

I would always remember homemade applesauce, sloppy joes, and the sweetness of fire-roasted s'mores. I knew Donna had no power over this dramatic situation and could imagine how she felt or how many times this had happened to her poor heart. It was something far greater than she could handle. I loved Donna and what she did to help those in need.

I was getting taken away from something close to happiness, and what peril awaited me on the other side was not a mystery. Group homes are something a child should never have to suffer through, especially so many times in such a short period.

Mike let me sit in the front seat of his SUV, and when I looked out the window, it was not just Donna crying and waving to me but all the kids too. John came running over to the car and handed me his Lakers jersey, smiling sadly. He was losing his little brother.

"I will never forget you, bro," he said with his head downcast.

Crying, I reached out to give him a fist bump. "Never," I said and didn't.

I felt even more of my innocence disappearing into a jungle of terror, far from Donna's comforting embrace. Driving away reminded me of losing my mother, handcuffed in front of our old house.

Was she okay? Was she alive or in prison?

There were no whispering jacaranda trees to send me off this time, and I had not seen one in a long time. Most of the trees around Donna's house were either pine or palm. She lived close enough to the ocean that I could smell it in the air.

I missed Donna and would have been happy living there for the rest of my childhood. I never saw her or John again.

ESPECIALLY FOR YOU,

Son

My Jeromy,

Though you're
a very special son
With fine and thoughtful ways,
Somehow it's all too seldom
That you get your share of praise —
That's why it's so important,
When a special day is here,
To remind you
that you're loved a lot
And wished the best all year.

Happy Birthday

I love you
very much
and miss you too.

Love
mom

P.S. I'll Be talking to
you soon.

CHAPTER 7

HUMILIATION

Orange, California, Spring 1987

—————————

Humility is the solid foundation of all virtues.
—CONFUCIUS

Dark memories of neglect filled my mind and hurt my heart. My social worker was required to get me checked out at the hospital.

Green tile, cold and damp from the shower, invited my tiny feet toward a porcelain demon who tormented me. My mother left the door unlocked this time, and I had already almost peed my pants. I had to go number two, so I stepped over her in childlike silence. She was sitting up by the built-in tub, eyes closed, with her head propped on a towel. Her arms spread out by each leg, and there was dried blood near her inside elbow.

Her breathing was slow, and a used needle lay next to her pale hand. It fell after she passed out, and I was careful to not step on it. A small glass pipe was resting on the tub edge, and her gorgeous hair covered most of her left side. Dark red nail polish had chipped off her fingers, and dark lipstick was worn thin on her dried-out lips. I could not tell if her eyes were completely closed, and it was scary.

●●●

I felt fear walking into CHOC (Children's Hospital of Orange County), a medical facility dedicated to helping kids.

My eyes misted over again. "Why are you taking me here, Mike?"

"We need to get you some help with your tummy, bud. Okay?"

"I don't want to go in there," I begged and did not understand.

Revolving doors with light blue–tinted glass swished gently as we walked into the cold hospital. That historic glass left tiny handprints all over, and I could see similar smudges at eye level. A cringing odor of ether hit my nose, and I felt another memory implode like a mental grenade from the past.

Trying to hold off the impending memory of my dad dying in a hospital bed was useless, and I was transported back. Transported to his beeping prison, next to his lonely metal bed, wondering if I could control my uncontrollable fear.

Instead of my cancer-riddled father in that thin bed, it was my mother this time. She looked dead, and I shook, unable to control the terror of her sunken eyes. She had the same tubes running through her but was lying in a green bathtub full of water instead of a hospital bed. She still had beautiful brown curly hair, but it tumbled lifelessly around her ashen face.

There was no vibrance of life in my memory, and I could see her maroon nails still chipped. There were no doctors and no visitors who cared. A TV showed static in the far corner, and it was weird seeing a bathtub in the middle of a hospital room.

Mike was leaning down in front of me with his hands on my shoulders, trying to calm me. I felt wetness all over my face from unabashed tears. I would never forget what had happened to my dad, and my imagination played horrible games with me. He held his hand out for me, and I took it without hesitation.

I was shaking from the vision of my mother, but resilience radiated from me, and I was not going to give up. Shadowed doors ahead of us beckoned.

Instead of chairs and sick people, the waiting area had toys, beanbags, and TVs playing cartoons. Murals of dinosaurs were drawn on the walls, and Mike let me roam around until it was time for my appointment. A nurse called my name, and I followed her away from the toys.

"Jeremy, I can't go with you, but I will be right here waiting until you get back," Mike said, kneeling in front of me.

I nodded, with my eyes downcast.

A scarecrow man in a white smock was waiting for me by a door that had no handle. His smile made his horn-rimmed glasses rise, and he was genuine in his care. The doctor leaned down a bit to ruffle my mop of curls and whispered something to Mike, who sat down in the waiting area.

I looked back, wishing he was coming with me, but his smile told me that he would be waiting for my return. The pediatrician led me down a fluorescent hallway that was so bright looking up caused temporary blindness. A big room that had double doors, with windows opened before us and a long metal bed in the middle of the room, took on a medieval presence.

A tall nurse was preparing items on some movable tray, and the ether of my nightmares was back. Sharp clinking of instruments pushed into my ears and squished my heart.

Her disarming smile put me at ease, but I had a strange feeling that something was not right—something was not good. The nurse handed me an olive-green hospital gown and pointed stoically at a curtained area for me to change behind. It was cold, and I could not stop shivering.

The pediatrician kindly picked me up and set me gently on the edge of the cloth-covered table. He gave me a hug and could not stop my tears.

"Jeremy, I understand you have had some tummy problems. How do you feel now?"

Intense pressure formed in my chest, and I, too, was scared to answer. I put my head on his chest and mumbled, "I just want my mommy."

The doctor stuttered a bit and said, "Jeremy, I am so sorry, but you must be brave now. Can you do that for me, please?"

I whispered, "Yes."

The doc's eyes were looking toward the ceiling. I noticed a large armlike device, with a crinkled hose attached, limply hanging down. He looked back at me as he put on a welder's mask and asked me to lie on my tummy.

The rest of this memory is blurred, and walking back to Mike's car was foggy.

●●●

Braking caused my head to roll forward, and I woke with a start. A large yellow home on the corner of an elevated street looked inviting, but I did not belong anywhere. I dreamed I was back with Donna and in a home that would never swallow me up again.

"Let's get you settled in before dinnertime, okay?" Mike said.

Extreme loneliness washed the hope out of me, and I was alone. My mother would never rescue me, and I knew that deep in my soul.

I had no one.

Hi sweetheart

Happy easter my
darling son I love
you very much and
the dream I have for
our future is a happy one.
Some day we will be
together. I know its hard
for you to believe right now
but I don't want drugs
in my life ever again. I
realize thats what brought
us apart and my darling
you are more important
to me than anything or
anyone you are my sunshine
and my reason for living.
I seem to keep missing
up but it doesn't lessen
my love for you. I've just
used very poor judgment
in things and I'm paying
for my mistakes. I'm so
sorry that things have
been so hard for you but
I will make it up to
you as soon as I can
    I love you with all
my heart & soul forever
keep up your good work
at school.
                always,
                mom

Here are
some
easter
things
to color

CHAPTER 8

HELP

Huntington Beach, California, 1987

────────────────

Oh, that I had wings like a dove! I would fly away and be at rest.
—PSALM 55:6 (NKJV)

Glowing tentacles of despair began to strangle the small amounts of energy I carried inside my weakened frame. The sapping effect was like a demon trying to demand entrance into my battered soul, but I was holding on to something deep inside that shook with rage at being tormented so. The intrepid anger became so hot it was cold and pushed back with such force the air permeated with crackling energy.

Hiding within myself, I slid further underneath the thin beige covers, trying to block out the nightmare weaving around me and failing miserably. The silence inside the desolate group home would have normally been a welcome retreat, had it not been tainted with the background sounds of the other kids happily splashing around in the small above-ground pool in the backyard.

Rigid pressure on my chest was a sickening reminder of the

gnarled fist of the demon still trying to break my willpower. My grip tightened around my weak layer of cotton protection as thoughts of my mother materialized before me. She was reaching out to me, calling for me, but every step she took forward sent her farther back into the fog. Tears began to puddle in my eyes, and I looked out the window for a sign of what was to come.

I could not see anything.

Soft beads of condensation melted down the inside of the paint-chipped window, creating liquid tracks that looked like the fanned limbs from a dead tree. The raspy air-conditioning blasted down off the window, right into my squinting eyes, and it made me shiver as I wiped away the mystic branches to see the road outside. An obtuse arch from my dampened hand slowly misted over again, and I was blinded from the world outside.

Child Help—my first group home, my first experience outside the orphanage, and the catalyst for which my life in the system would begin.

A few days before, I had been dropped off by Mike, and I was just a number in the cog of kids hidden within the constructs of the legal system.

●●●

Settled on the rounded corner of two intersecting streets, within the maze of suburbia in Huntington Beach, the Child Help group home was a one-story rambler with dull orange tile shingles. If one paid close enough attention to the school buses that parked directly in front of the house every morning or afternoon, the lack of children playing outside, and the steady stream of adults flowing in and out, suspicion might arise.

This was no normal family home.

I remember hearing the social worker's parking brake engage with an oily screech to keep the car from moving on the inclined driveway. A feeling of terror slowly pulled me from the car, and my feet refused to cooperate. I could taste blood in my mouth from biting the inside of my cheek too hard.

I was shaking in fear when we began the treacherous walk up the pavement toward the angry front door. It was luminous in front of me, and I could hear the whisper of a horror anthem grating in the background or inside my imagination.

"Jeremy, are you okay, buddy?" Mike asked while guiding me toward my unavoidable demise. He knew I was scared; he knew I knew there was no going back from this point, and we both understood the abyss beyond this otherworldly door was something no child should ever have to endure.

I nodded slowly, with my head downcast, shaking curly hair out to hide my ethereal tears. Palm trees leaned in with their judgment and pointed at me with their shadows. They sensed my isolation and fear.

A rhythmic booming sound invaded my senses, causing me to see through the curly strands hiding my sadness. Mike was knocking on the wavering door, and it felt like each time his fist touched the wood, it sunk in like a rock in tar and shook the rippled world around me.

Hiding quickly behind his leg, I waited for the echoing footsteps to get closer and for the trolls to eat me alive. There was even a long, grating squeak from the door hinges as it opened inwardly to expose the keeper within. Craning my neck to see the monster, I only noticed an awkward smile and a massive red beard.

It really was a monster.

The monster lumberjack had the same color hair on his arms as his beard, and his teal flannel shirt contrasted greatly with pale white skin. His pronounced bent nose sat under black beady eyes. They might have been blue. My robust imagination portrayed him as an evil creature who eats tasty children at his front door like morsels of chocolate.

Time was still a fragmented mess, and it was hard to remember my separation from Mike and my struggle with the lumberjack, but the darkness beyond never brightened. If there was any light that warmed my skin, it was the thought of seeing my mother again and the need to fight for every step.

Crippling gloom tortured my battered senses, and I immediately felt the deep silence of the home weighing down on my loneliness. I was walking into an inanimate box that held only wicked memories because there was nothing truly good or whole to hold on to.

Each creaking footstep destroyed my innocent freedom and took me farther from the family who left me behind. The lumberjack tried unsuccessfully to hold my trembling hand; I kept jerking it away in a vain attempt at defiance.

"Please don't make me go in there," I whispered to Mike.

He was already backing up toward where his car was parked. "I will be back in a few days to check on you, buddy," Mike said and got in his car quickly.

I nodded, with my head down, and looked back toward the dungeon.

The lumberjack's smile held menace, and the viselike grip he found around my wrist allowed the monster to drag me toward a room in the back with ease. I slid around like a mop on the oyster-colored linoleum floor, wondering if this was my life now. I kicked my feet around for added emphasis. We had stopped in front of the last of three bedrooms, and all I could hear was the lumberjack's panting.

"Jeremy, I don't want to fight with you. The bed on the right is yours, and I will be back in a bit to check on you." The lumberjack huffed, with his hand resting on the doorjamb for support.

"Where are all the other kids?" I asked softly.

His hunched back turned away as he trudged along back down the narrow hall and haphazardly garbled over his shoulder, "They are at school, Jeremy, and will be back this afternoon."

Sweet rays of light squeezed through the dimpled holes of condensation on the one window in my room, and it rose to tickle my face as I searched for a sense of belonging in a world that held no mercy. I felt the warmth of the sun resting gently on the top of my hand and in the synthetic fibers of the carpet entwined through my fingers.

Hidden gems of solace sparkled inside the bed sheets and reached out to me in unexpected comfort. I quickly found myself within their tentlike shelter, shaking with fear of the unknown. I dreamed my mother would take me from this wretched place. Where was she?

Peeking through the plush triangle of light that emitted radiantly from my protective fort, I saw my window within a window. The combination of unknown fear and the simple curiosity of seeing what was outside gave way to me melting out of the sheets and peering through that dewy glass.

Colorless fiends of discontent hovered outside my new prison, lethargically waiting for me to join their soulless journey and to obediently follow them into miserable darkness. Spirits searching for souls of the lost, they congregated outside my window in hopes that my youthful innocence would disintegrate into potent hate.

Unfortunately for them, I would survive and resist.

Tearing my eyes away from the imaginary fools outside, I boldly sought the red-haired monster by peeking out of the dungeon and sneaking to the end of the antechamber. I remember seeing the front door beckoning me, but my fear of getting caught was greater. I heard squeaking footsteps on linoleum and voices of kids in another room. I pattered back to my cell on silent feet and loud fear.

The lumberjack's bearlike head tugged at a lumbering body to enter my room without banging hunched shoulders into the door panel. I could see him staring at my bed from under the covers. He knocked gently on the wall before speaking. "Um, Jeremy, would you like to meet the rest of the kids and staff members? They are all at the kitchen table getting ready for dinner," he asked in a loud whisper.

Was it that late already? I thought Mike had just dropped me off. Maybe I fell asleep and was watching myself stare at the demons outside. The blurring of time forced my silence, and I feared ignoring him.

"I'm scared and just want to be alone," I whispered.

I saw his body relax, like me speaking was a miracle. His

shuffling gait stated clearly that he still felt awkward comforting children. He sat down next to me and touched my foot gently before patting it. "Come on out to the dining room, bud, so you can meet everyone."

"All right," I whispered pathetically.

Five other kids were sitting at the table in silence. They stared at me without good intentions, and I could tell they were more interested in my embarrassment than my comfort.

I don't remember any of them. Their torture and humiliation suffocated my existence. Every single day, I was the object of their filthy curiosity, and there was no night I slept soundly. There was no hiding, and they found me, no matter where I tried to run.

● ● ●

Silence seeped out of the old carpet and into the fabric of my being, quickly shooting goose bumps up my arms, making me shiver. I was a foreigner in my room, and it was hard to move away from the glossy window, where I felt somewhat safe. If I touched anything, it would mean I lived there, and I wanted for just that moment to forget how alone I was.

A low, rumbling car drove by, waking me from what would be a short-lived safety net. My innate terror of not knowing what was going to happen next kept vigil inside my being and watched with keen eyes. I felt shaking all through my body, and my legs gave up on the wasted effort of standing. Something innate pulled me down into the forlorn wall next to the dresser under the window, and the shaking transformed into ghoulish shadows jumping to the ceiling.

Lethargically, I moved back onto the bed and laid my exhausted mane of curls on the pillow, leaving the blanket pile untouched. They should just leave me alone.

I must have fallen asleep. A sleep that draws the tears inside and keeps them hidden from the evil that wonders therein. Peace overcame me in this world of wishes, but I knew it was imaginary and would only be a short reprieve of what was to come. What was to come?

I was alienated at Child Help, which was more like Child Hell. It was apparent I was a temporary object waiting to be moved. While other children played outside in the pool, I stayed in my room and felt alone. It was an everyday journey that caused me deep emotional trauma, and my stomach problems continued.

Instead of helping me, this group home hurt me. I celebrated my seventh birthday at Child Help, but there is no memory. There was no celebration.

The fear of using the restroom embarrassed me. My ability to withstand the verbal abuse from the other kids usually ended with tears. This brought more torture, and for some reason the staff members never seemed to be there to intervene. My resolve was slowly breaking apart; my mother was never coming back, and the thought of watching all the other kids go home with family on the weekends while I stayed was a white-hot pain embedded inside my bones.

School memories existed only as partial images. The stomach trouble followed me to school, where I would hold it all day. I remember coming home and having to do the unimaginable.

My room felt alive with agitation, and before me stood a large white man with larger eyes and a mean presence. He was wearing jeans and a white polo shirt, but his skin was almost the color of the shirt. I knew what was coming, and when he led me toward the bathroom, I began to cry. He was a giant.

"Please don't make me do this again," I begged.

Bleach stung my bloodshot eyes, and tears poured down my reddened face from clenched fear. The echoing bathroom was dank, and I was so scared that my constant shivering made it hard for me to kneel. My dirty underwear was in the toilet, and since they had skid marks, I had to wash them out by hand.

The giant locked me in there with only my hands to do the work, and I could hear him grumbling outside the door. I had no idea what enraged him, so I remained silent and stood in my bath towel, which upset him more.

"Hurry up in there. Other kids need to use the bathroom," the giant bellowed. It was the only bathroom kids could use, and every time this happened, the giant was the one to enslave me.

My equilibrium was off, and my little hands burned. The tile was cold on my legs, and I knew this was just the beginning of a battle that would test the strength of my will. I stood up and looked over at the door in uncertainty.

"Um, I am all done now," I croaked, looking down at my red hands that would soon crack from the cleaning solution.

He was in my face before the door opened all the way and had pushed my neck down toward the toilet. He made me take the underwear out of the toilet with my hands, ring them out, and then put them in the bathtub to rinse out. I tried to move quickly so I would not upset him more. When I looked behind me, I saw two of the older boys pointing at me with large grins on their faces.

The giant turned on the shower and looked at me with a hideous expression.

"Get in that shower and clean yourself off right now."

The towel that was wrapped around my tiny waist was the only thing that I could hide in, and the door was still open for everyone to see. I looked back and tried to muster enough strength to take it off, but I couldn't.

When my eyes found his, they were full of red anger, and he pushed me toward the steaming shower while simultaneously pulling off the towel. In an instant, it was ripped off me, and large hands were underneath my armpits, lifting me into the scalding hot water. I was half tossed into the bathtub, banging my shoulder into the built-in green soap holder and slipping clumsily before the giant slammed the curtains closed.

I could feel each burning bead of water like a decontamination bath, and the giant's shadow loomed outside the curtain while he paced around. His breathing was demonic, and I tried to hurry before his unchecked rage bellowed out again.

The giant let the kids pee while I was in the shower, and every one of them mumbled under their breath. They hated me and enjoyed ganging up on me.

My chemical-stained towel was hanging over the rusty curtain bar, and I was barely tall enough to grab the end, but I managed to jump for it without slipping.

That would not be the only time the giant threw me in the bleached cesspool. He never called me Jeremy—only dirty boy. Other kids didn't have this as punishment, but none had my problems. They all knew of my issue, and it segregated me further from all the activities in the group home.

Not a single kid there acted as a friend. The group home staff seemed content to let me wallow in my cell and not deal with me. On weekends, I came out when they offered meals. It kept me from starving.

The quiet kept the giant from me and allowed me to feel something other than fear.

Through this neglect, I had more problems using the restroom, and the constant torment from the Child Help staff members would only got worse. This group home seemed to have favorites, and the staff made it painfully obvious I was not on the list.

Kids made fun of me profusely and ganged up on me, beating me up. Their favorite time was when we waited for the school bus; there was no getting away. Through swollen lips, Child Help inadvertently taught me the meaning of keeping my mouth shut and staying out of sight.

Usually, Christmas was a time of giving and family. For children, it is the thought of a big red Santa bumbling down the chimney and perfect snowflakes falling outside. All the while, the child opens up huge presents they had been wanting all year. With closed eyes, that is what a group home kid sees. With them open, I was the only one who remained behind for Christmas 1987.

I almost gave up on life after that gloomy Christmas. I thought of ways to stop existing. I hoped I wouldn't wake up. It was worse than being alone, and my heart was broken.

My courage to continue dwindled, and I found reasons to not eat or even drink water. I would never try to hurt myself or anything, but maybe if I stopped eating, I could disappear. The pain was too great. The loneliness too severe. The not knowing if I would ever be saved too hard to bear.

When was this dragon of darkness finally going to swallow my breaking heart?

Then a miracle came. His name was Robert "Bob" Butler, and he became my court-appointed special advocate (CASA). He was my savior and kicked away the loneliness. From the moment I met him, I trusted him. I think from the moment he saw me, he knew we were meant to meet. I think of him now, and my heart hurts with love for him.

Bob came to me when my mother was in jail or gone, my real father was dead, and those families left me for reasons unknown. My thoughts of family resembled darkly lit fantasies. He was my only visitor and the only one who knew how broken my heart was.

Bob was my strength, my friend, and my guiding light.

The day he found me, I was lost. And the day he found me, I had given up.

The menacing dragon of darkness did not come back.

CHAPTER 9

SAVIOR

Huntington Harbour, California, 1988

———————

More and more, when I single out the person who inspired me most,
I go back to my grandfather.
—JAMES EARL JONES

The sun's gentle kiss was hidden partially by water-soaked beams, holding the porch together. Shimmering reflections inside a small puddle, teeter-tottering on the dull blue banister, held chipped blue paint. It flaked off the stucco walls outside and settled in a pile on the gray cement floor. I could feel the previous night's rain between my toes as I walked barefoot toward a kind old man sitting at the white plastic table outside.

His appearance radiated energy, and deep-set blue eyes gleamed from afar. He reminded me of comfortable cotton, strength, and kindness. I felt an instant connection, and his smile made the burden of loneliness dissipate.

His hand, which had a purple bruise, rested on a board game, and his other hand cupped a folded knee. The staff member was oblivious to our eye contact and never realized the great man in front of us would keep me safe. He wore a light blue button-down shirt that looked like it had been worn hundreds of times, and he smiled with a wave of his hand.

His crisp shirt pocket was stuffed with a glasses case and a gold pen. Countless crinkles around his eyes showed how much he smiled, and the sun beamed off perfectly combed silver hair.

"You must be Jeremy," he said, his big hand out to shake.

When I took it, mine looked like a small child's doll in his. His voice was steady, deep, and held wisdom that I wanted to listen to all day.

"My name is Bob," he said kindly and patted my hand before pointing to the chair next to him.

"Hi, Bob, what's that?" I asked, pointing at the game and sitting right where he asked.

He placed the game between us. "This? It's called *Parcheesi*. Ever heard of it?" Bob asked.

Before I could respond, he opened it to show me the colorful pastel pieces, slowly explaining what the game was and seeing how I responded. Instantly, I was hooked.

Bob was there to take me away from the darkness.

I started softly crying. I tried to stop before he thought I wasn't brave. Someone put me first and paid attention to me. I couldn't control the emotion pouring from my heart. My tears formed huge reflective streams down my face, and my breath caught in my quivering throat.

An odd situation for Bob, but his understanding of my pain connected us, and he put his hand on my shoulder. He didn't say anything and just let me cry.

His hands were rough and calloused from work as a flight-testing engineer for McDonnell Douglas, later bought out by Boeing. Those hands were safe, and he didn't even know how close I had come to giving up.

"Here, Jeremy, take my handkerchief." He handed me a soft white cloth that he let me keep.

"I can learn fast," I told him through tears, mesmerized by his kindness.

That day was etched in my heart. It was the day I didn't have to fight alone. Bob gave his most valuable gift—his time. The second time he came to visit, I knew it was real. It was not a one-time deal, and he didn't care about what others made fun of me for. His ability to open the clouds of despair and shine a light that decimated my sadness was profound.

He would enter the home and bring happiness into my dreary heart. Bob brought me doughnuts and happiness every Saturday. He knew how they treated me. I lived for weekends now, and no other time mattered, just the day my Bob would come. On some weekends, he would bring me gifts like board games, puzzles, or even a G.I. Joe I told him I liked. He remembered things like that, and I could not fathom how I got so lucky.

I never told the other kids what I was given and hid everything so they would not beat me up and steal it. They still found the gifts, so I asked Bob to keep them in his truck. He didn't even question it.

My fear of the giant lingered daily, but now I was not a number in a group home.

"How old are you, Jeremy?" he asked me one morning as he taught me chess on a small travel board that looked like it had been around since his kids were small.

"Seven," I said.

"Perfect! I think we will go see a movie today. How does that sound?"

"Really!?" I almost screamed.

I had never been to a movie theater. I was overwhelmed again, and tears filled my eyes. When I looked away, it was because I didn't want him to think I was a crybaby.

I felt his hand on my shoulder again, and he let me collect myself. There was no judgment, and he walked me to the passenger side of his awesome Ford truck.

"Can I come live with you?" I asked.

"I wish you could, pal," he answered, his voice slow and sad.

Quiet authority surrounded him, and he had an unwavering moral compass. I asked him question after annoying question, and he was patient with me every time. His intelligence was profound, and he knew the answers to everything.

Bob's tan-colored Ford Ranger smelled like sunburned plastic, engine oil, and Old Spice. I loved it and him, with all my heart. He was my cornerstone, mentor, and who I would want my father to be, if I had one.

Even when the coastal wind blew, his hair was a perfect wave cresting gray and white over his head. Deep wrinkles, like granite fissures on the side of a mountain, connected happy smile lines at the corner of his mouth and radiated kindness. The endearing power in which he stood made me trust him, and he didn't even know it.

After a month or so of visiting me in the group home or at a movie nearby, I was allowed to stay the night at his home in Huntington Beach. On that day, he kept it a secret, and I believed we were going to another movie.

After a longer than normal drive, I asked him, "Hey, Bob, where we were going?"

The glint in his eyes matched his big smile. He was wearing a light blue polo with a pocket on the chest holding his glasses case, and a silver-colored watch glistened while he held the worn steering wheel.

"It was a secret, but I am taking you to my home, and you can meet my wife, Bella."

The maiden drive to his home was mesmerizing and felt like a dream. I could not contain my excitement and asked him ridiculous, annoying questions the whole time.

"Where are we, Bob?" I asked when we drove down a beautiful street that followed the ocean. I had never been around this part of the water.

"It's called Huntington Harbour," he said with a soft smile, and I could tell he loved that place.

His Ranger stopped in front of a gorgeous end-unit townhome, and a gentle older woman was out front, watering blooming birds-of-paradise. She had on one of those long, flowery dresses that only grandmas wore, and I could feel her love from afar.

When I got out, I didn't know what to do and just stood there, awestruck. She was also a CASA and knew of my struggle.

"You must be Jeremy," she said sweetly as I held on to the truck door. She came right over and wrapped me in a huge grandma hug. It was impossible not to cry again, but I tried. This couldn't be real.

I was in shock and held in my tears as best as I could.

"My name is Ines, but everyone in this big family calls me Bella, and you are now part of it. Does that sound good to you?" she said while guiding me toward the front door with her soft, motherly hand on my back.

Bob was strolling ahead toward the house, and I ran after him, slipping my little hand in his. I could not go a second without him close by. He instantly closed his calloused hands around mine and took me up to the white door to another world. A wooden sign read, "The Butlers," and I wanted to be part of it.

A beautiful piano was pushed up against the wall in the entry-way, and a huge two-story living room that had perfect white carpet greeted me. In that living room, above the huge fireplace, was a very strange yet mesmerizing portrait of a Renaissance man. His eyes followed me everywhere.

Taking my shoes off at the door was a requirement. Bob showed me around while Bella went to their galley-style kitchen, continuing her magical homemade pasta sauce. She was Sicilian, and so was I, which gave us an instant bond. I had never had homemade Italian food before but would get the chance. This was not some chunky meat sauce. This was a beautifully smooth red sauce that smelled like restaurant heaven on a velvety red-sauce road that ended in my salivating mouth. Every inhale of that decadent aroma had me floating toward the kitchen like Tom and Jerry stealing a fruity pie from a cartoon kitchen window.

Bella timed cooking perfectly, and when Bob finished showing me the room I would stay in upstairs, she had our food piled high.

"*Mangia*, Jeremy, *mangia*," she said while putting more mostaccioli on my already heaping plate. It was like penne without the lines, twice the size so I could scoop up all that saucy goodness, and perfectly al dente.

We sat together at the old, round wooden table I would come to love, and I couldn't imagine sleeping over. I was not in a group home.

"Jeremy, do you like golf?" Bob asked stoically between mouthfuls.

"Umm, I don't know what that is," I said, hoping I didn't say the wrong thing.

Pouring vodka from a plastic bottle into a small glass with ice, he smiled down at me and said, "Let me show you on the boob tube."

"What's a boob tube?" I asked as he led me to his den, which was connected to the kitchen.

Laughing so loud it made me laugh, Bob said, "Oh, Jeremy, that is the TV."

We sat together for hours, each on our own couch, and I realized very quickly we were filling a void each had. His relationship with his sons seemed distant, and I think he was making up for times that as a father were hard. I was lucky to be given this chance, and I would forever be grateful.

We did that every single weekend.

Just me and Bob, watching movies, sitting around watching golf, and hanging out together all weekend. He never once got annoyed with my relentless questions, and he always put me first.

Some of my fondest memories are of him taking me from the group home, driving to Winchell's Donuts, and getting chocolate-covered long Johns. The movie section of the folded newspaper opened before us, and it was so fun figuring out which two movies we would be watching. Yes, we theater hopped, and it was glorious.

Back then, one could watch back-to-back movies without getting caught, since the seats were not assigned. One could sneak in early before the theater staff asked for a ticket.

As my life began to look up, and I had a friend who cared about me, I should have known it was time for another dark catalyst.

●●●

I hadn't seen my social worker, Mike, in a long time. Yet there he was, a day before Bob was coming to take me to a movie.

"Hey, Jeremy," he greeted me. His brown blazer looked wrinkled from driving, and his hair seemed thinner.

"Hi, Mike," I answered with my head down.

"Hey, buddy, how are you doing?" he asked.

"Okay, how are you?" I replied.

"Well, I got some rough news for you, so I am not feeling that great, to be honest." We sat outside at the same table where I learned to play games with Bob.

"Let me guess—Orangewood," I whispered under my breath.

Stuttering and shifting, he said, "Yes, I am so sorry, Jeremy."

"I'm not. So why should you care?" I said softly, and tears came swiftly to my eyes.

"Why can't they just leave me alone? Why can't I just go back with my mom or Bernie? I want to live with Bob, but that is not possible," I said, not caring if I was heard.

"Bob can still visit you, Jeremy, and that is the good news," he said with sadness. "I called him this morning, and he knows what is happening. Don't worry—he will make sure you are okay and will drive you there."

I took a deep breath and smiled it away. Maybe everything in my meager existence was only partially flattened. Bob was going to pick me up and take me to see an awesome movie while letting me stuff my face with doughnuts one last time. He was sad for me and had not been to Orangewood until that fateful moment.

Time shifted again. That weekend was a distant memory, and the journey from Huntington Beach heaven to the City of Orange hell began coldly. Bob would not think differently of me, but it was hard to imagine driving to a prison and him wanting to see me again.

"Jeremy, have you been here before?" Bob asked as we parked in front of the brick castle my terrors were born of. He looked pale and sad.

I just nodded and started to cry uncontrollably, breathing funny and heaving. He held me until I settled and waited even longer because the shock of his Jeremy getting stuffed back into a child prison hurt him to the core.

"I am going to be here every weekend to come to see you," he said softly.

But I knew once I was in there, the fake plastic couches were the only place to visit—no weekend outings. "You promise?" I asked.

Bob nodded with a sad smile.

My prison was waiting.

Despair took over the light as the day faded coldly, and there was no sunset. The breeze died with me as we walked to the intake office. Bob was only allowed in the front office, and they placed my stuff in a container that went into some locked cabinet.

He gave me a strong hug and told me, "Jeremy, don't you ever change. You are special, and we will get through this together."

I hugged him back and cried. It didn't matter. The demons inside would exploit my weaknesses and beat the happiness out of me.

I watched him walk out the door as it reflected the bright setting sun and painted his shadow toward me. I was alone again.

●●●

I took my place back in the preteen ward at Orangewood. Nice nail lady was not there, but everything looked the same. The veritable closet had the same old clothes, and I went through the exact intake process. Bob was only allowed to see me in the sanitized family meeting area. He witnessed firsthand the torment, the isolation, and the sterile way of living.

This went on for over six months, the longest I ever stayed at that hell on earth. My mother was missing in action and had not called or written. Each day was a fight. A fight against the demons of loneliness and the warlocks of self-pity.

The twisted months went by slowly. Bob was the only thing that kept me alive. I heard nothing about my family and had no idea if I would ever get out of this place. Bernie never came, nor did Aunt Sherie or anyone on my father's side.

Bella came a few times, as she was also a well-respected CASA and knew Orangewood. It broke her gentle heart to see me there, so it was not every time.

Bob would bring my favorite doughnuts, and we would play a board game or cards. He loved hearts and gin rummy, but I think what he loved most was giving me hope.

He sacrificed his time on the weekends to see me, and it did give me that hope. I wanted him to be proud of me for not giving up and staying happy.

The dejected dogs howling to the moon next door at the pound were the only familial noises I felt drawn to at night. I silently cried into a flat yellow pillow, hoping to not get beat up the next day.

La Bicyclette Fleurie
Kyrie

CHAPTER 10

SILENCE

Orange, 1988

━━━━━━━━━━

When words become unclear, I shall focus with photographs. When images become inadequate, I shall be content with silence.
—ANSEL ADAMS

I turned eight within the sticky web of Orangewood Children's Foundation and didn't say a word, nor did they. By this point, I had been there longer than anyone else. That did not change the torment or the worry of getting beat up or harassed.

Why would anyone care how old I was in an institution that had so many children it could not contain? I was another damaged, half-breed repeat delinquent who could not even make it in a "caring" group home. A kid who came crawling back to that which he was spawned. Past the same clinical entrance, along the dangerous path toward brutal beatings and horrible situations.

That is what awaited me like spiders in the darkness.

My battered emotions felt as tired as the sweeping jacaranda trees of foggy dreams past. Heroine addicted, my mother was probably lost to the disease and had not once even called to see if I was okay. Poor, noble Bob, my only lifeline, was given an hour on Sunday to see me. He still came—he still visited, no matter what.

My poor mom was still in my heart. She was not an abusive parent; I knew she loved me, but with drug addiction, that was not enough motivation to beat it. Even my social worker had no idea where she was.

● ● ●

The first bloody beatdown came by way of rusty bicycle chains, right after a traumatizing frozen-pea lunch, on a tree-shaded sidewalk layered with gravel.

A quiet place I had previously felt safe due to the patrolling staff members was now open season for bullies. I was pushed into the bushes so hard my shins hit the low-rise brick planter, and I tumbled face-first. I felt blood trickling down my legs.

"Get his little bitch feet!" I heard one of the assailants squawk.

"Let's get him," another said viciously.

I felt the side of my head hit the planter bricks before I was thrown to the ground. My head bounced a few times on the ground as they dragged me away from the view of the staff. Gravel was everywhere, and it kicked up a plume of gray dust that caked around my eyes.

Iron chains hit my legs, back, and arms, in an unorganized dance of pain lasting forever.

"How does that feel, you little bitch?" another boy said.

They knew how it felt, as I could not control my screaming and crying. Bullies were a normal day-to-day threat at Orangewood, and I was an easy target.

"Stop hitting me! Stop it, please!" I screamed, knowing it didn't matter.

The big tree and bushes blocked the staff members' field of vision. Other kids looked on in amusement, happy in their bliss it wasn't them getting smacked with chains.

Powerful silence drew me back to the present and to my blood-soaked reality. I saw the group of bullies by the preteen ward doors staring at me with menace. That look would manifest into more beatdowns and torment.

Blood trickled down my back, and I felt shame. By the time I limped to the door, a staff member noticed I was hurt. She took me quietly to the nurse, who was the same lady as before.

"Jeremy, what happened?" she questioned me.

I stayed silent, and I would not rat. I knew going to the nurse would get around anyway. The nurses' station was between the preteen wards. It smelled like baby powder and had crayon drawings all over the walls.

Knocked down by life, I never gave up, and it was a big part of my character. There was never a moment when I could not make myself smile or laugh.

Intrepid investigations allowed me to find new secret locations not frequented by bullies and away from the rebellious teens who haunted the foundation walls. My favorite was a shadowy alcove built around the side of the church that was hidden from view by big pine trees and another building that could have been used for storage but looked like a park bathroom.

At night, when the shuffling sounds of staff member footsteps became robotic echoes cascading the hallways, I would dream of my mother. I would dream of being saved, happily watching the always lurking pimpled faces of the bullies as my mother, on a red carpet, would walk in like an actress, pulling me toward freedom.

There would be sublime moments during the darkest of the night or the earliest of the morning, before the world would wake up, that I would have a great escape idea. It would slip away before the lights turned on. This never manifested into anything other than hopelessness and a sad realization that even running away was impossible.

Then I would have nightmares. The good dream was a prelude to the impossible fear. Those obscure thoughts within my sleep were always lurking to punish me at night.

Hearing the clicks of hospital-style lights turning on was like automatic doors to a prison. It made my heart race upon waking up in a white cell. That sound—the sharp snapping of multiple switches being flicked on quickly—led to chaos in the bleached hallways beyond.

It was the same during the nightly routine, only sprinkled with a few punches and shoves into walls. It was a cycle that gave little in the way of assurance or safety.

Reality was the great equalizer in this windowless orphanage. I wasn't going anywhere, and nobody was coming to save me. The only way to get through the torment was to stay positive. Never give up or give in. I had to see past the weakness that was being the victim.

"Watch out today, you little faggot," came a nasally whisper to my right.

I had just walked out of my room, waiting to fall into line for our daily clothes allotment. The blazing lights above still made my eyes see bright rings, but I knew that voice, and it scared me. Anger radiated from him.

This happened every day, and I began to understand the wisdom of silence. My tormentor was a heavyset, small-headed white kid who towered over me. He found ways to humiliate me in front of everyone, and the other kids laughed their fake laughs.

A group laugh created by their own fear. They were doing everything possible to stay away from the big menace. He loved beating me up and seeing the reactions from those who were similarly cruel, which were many.

I hid my fear and said nothing. This infuriated Small Head and quickly taught me to not ingest others' negativity. If I didn't accept it, their darkness stayed with them, infecting every part of their being and keeping them hidden in unhappiness.

Small Head would smack me or shove me, but my lack of response sent him into fits of rage.

Learn from those who talk a lot, but don't say anything. Learn from those who are loud, but speak nonsense. This was my introduction to the wisdom of silence, understanding balance, and how to manipulate the world in my favor without hurting anyone.

One morning Small Head flung syrup at me during breakfast. He was loud, obnoxious, and one of the most recognizable bullies at Orangewood. I evaded him during the morning routines of getting clothes and brushing teeth. During breakfast, he maneuvered in the serving line so that we would sit at the same large table.

Small Head was the first asshole who taught me to think ahead, watch what happens, and learn how to outsmart those who think they are better than you. Pretending to sit right before him, I stalled until he sat, and I got up, moving to the table behind me before another kid could take the seat.

The distance was good, and I was not facing him, but he could still throw things at me or make snide comments.

I held a dark fear close, and it was from getting beat up constantly. Small Head's beady eyes on me caused the hairs on my neck to rise, goose bumps to splay across my arms, and it threw shivers down my spine. Nothing could take my resolve.

"I know you hear me, you little bitch," Small Head said, loud enough for me but not the staff members nearby. I could hear him, but not registering his hollow bravado was an internal victory. My hands were shaking, so I hid them under the table and kept my eyes downcast.

I was pulled backward, and my knees hit the underside of the table, knocking over a bunch of juice cups. I hit my head hard on the dirty tile floor, and laughter emanated around me. My shoulder blades hurt from landing on the small plastic chair weirdly, and tears were in my eyes from the embarrassment.

I got up a little slower this time and smelled the syrup caked all over my back. It didn't matter that everyone was staring or whispering; all that mattered was to walk away, head held high.

I picked up the chair and pushed it back in respectfully. "I'm sorry," I told the kids who got juice on them from my fall.

"Jeremy, are you okay?" a familiar voice said sweetly behind me a short while later.

"I'm okay," I said, trying not to cry more. The smell of syrup permeated my nose, and I didn't want to look up in case the tears in my eyes got worse.

"Let's get you cleaned up, and then you can go relax in the common area," she said with a question in her voice.

"Okay," I whispered with resignation. I knew Small Head would be nearby. He always found me.

"Do you know who pushed you over, Jeremy?" she asked, knowing I would say the same thing.

"No, I didn't see them," I said.

She left it at that and gently pushed me along to the boys' showers, where I could wash my hair and get a new change of clothes.

• • •

The feeling of warm sunlight kissing my skin was a brief respite from the cold biting into my isolated soul. Its depth was a frozen apocalyptic wasteland that battered against a wall of tenacity, leaking out black tentacles of loneliness through pores of doubt. My flimsy self-worth was attached to that doubt, like trails of smoke from a chimney in winter, and quickly melted into what remained of my willingness to care.

I didn't care anymore, and I knew it was wrong to feel that way. My moral compass battled against giving in. Give in to being bad like all the other kids and follow the easy path. It could be fun to act like Small Head, to finally have a group of friends instead of the stark loneliness I saw in the dirty bathroom mirrors every morning.

My soul fought against that, and I wanted to vomit at the thought of hurting others to make myself look cool. I would never be like that young tyrant or his troop of turds.

Some days I escaped torture and found a short reprieve. I felt the sun sweetly burn into my mane of curly hair, and the power of peace radiated throughout me. It was not every day, but I tried my best to evade rough situations.

Days bled together at Orangewood, and my feeble memory closed off many uncomfortable moments at Orangewood. Running away bubbled up as a dark thought of escape, surviving and living outside the sickening embrace of isolation.

The staff at Orangewood took more notice of me based on always doing what was asked and never talking back. Doing the right thing was a testament to who I was and wanted to be.

Bob was always there on weekends. He gave me a moment of humanity and reminded me I was not alone in this world. In those few hours, hope found me and gave me the resolve to make it another week. Bob brought happiness and doughnuts, but just enough for our visit so the Small Heads of Orangewood wouldn't steal my treat.

Sometimes he would bring a book to read while I did word searches or looked at the comics out of the newspaper he brought. It was miserable seeing ads for cool movies, but I knew Bob enjoyed learning, so I did the puzzles. The staff began to give us more space and even let me sit out front of Orangewood on the few picnic benches.

"Jeremy, you can call me grandpa, like my other grandkids," he said one day.

I just hugged him tight and knew if I spoke, I would cry.

The bullies found me again, the same day Grandpa came with delicious doughnuts. That Saturday he came early and had to drive after that visit to see his daughter in nearby Aliso Viejo.

I was hiding in one of my secret locations behind the church in a low-lit niche. They knew I was there and had been watching. Five of them came in and held me down.

This time they picked me and threw me in a trash can. Pushing me down, they kicked the can over and started rolling me.

I kicked out hard and screamed, "No! Stop!" until they ran off laughing. I got out of the trash and had gross liquids all over me. They found my favorite hideout, and I was running out of options. Nobody could watch hundreds of kids, or understand which ones were the bullies, as they acted like saints to the staff.

Swiftly getting back to the preteen ward and smelling of old milk, I asked the staff to take me to the showers. I did not cry or tell, and they didn't ask what had happened.

● ● ●

It was not all horror and terror at Orangewood.

There was a big gym, with coaches who put together cool events for the children. We balanced peacock feathers on our noses, jumped around on red bouncy balls with handles, and played a fun game called wipeout. The bullies were rarely involved, and that was perfect.

Orangewood promoted creative learning, and I took to art very quickly.

I had a knack for drawing and was allowed to participate in

many of the older kids' classes. I did this even though it was just an opportunity for them to pick on me. The jealous ones who picked on me didn't like that the teacher complimented me on my drawing.

Of all the artistic memories, one stood out. The teacher taught us to make animals from the alphabet. There was something so fun from that exercise that it stayed with me.

A for ant, *B* for bear, *C* for cat, *D* for dog, *E* for elephant, and so on. Briefly, I felt normal and could pretend I was like any other kid going to school.

Another memory was the Orangewood behavioral system.

My name was usually first and held all gold stars. I took pride in doing the right thing, even when that meant getting beat up. Across the top of the chart was the name of the child and vertically down to the left were daily requirements. Anything from chores, making beds, getting things done on time to being kind and helpful was on there.

The staff would treat us better when we did the right things.

"Jeremy B., Gold star today for helping mop floors and cleaning up food in the cafeteria," said the director one time.

I sat by myself under the arm of a pleather couch, in the back of the bleach-smelling room, and smiled. There was snickering and laughter from a group of kids by the wall of windows looking out toward the dog pound. They were proud of their red stars and loved to make fun of the boy who they considered a suck-up.

It was survival.

"Broccoli" or "Brontosaurus" were the easy ones, but it was always something that led to kids being mean. "Broccoli head gets another gold star," the red stars teased before the staff members quieted them down.

Those moments were hard. They hurt me, and I had no friends or anyone willing to even sit next to me. The loneliness from that allowed me to find solace in the presence of adults. I began to spend all my time around the staff members, who quickly included me in their everyday interactions.

Some of the staff members, and even the director, would allow me to become a little hideaway rug rat. No other kids were given that type of attention, and they worked hard at not making it obvious so I would not get beaten up by the red stars.

One warm Southern California day, right after a rare barbecue in the pavilion area, I met the Saint.

All the red stars had gone to recess to enjoy the sun at its zenith or pick on another kid. I was allowed to stay behind due to my emotional connection to many of the staff members. They protected me from other kids during the day, so it was not different than the rest. Sometimes they would share their lunches with me or give me extra fries from their fast-food meals.

Not far behind me, where the staff members' offices were and the main door leading to the outside of Orangewood, excited voices emerged. I turned around, not realizing or thinking anything could be for me. One of the staff members was pointing in my direction, and the Saint walked toward me with a contagious confidence.

It was not my amazing Bob Butler, but another Bob. Bob Ford, the man who took me away from hell, in a white minivan. The Saint owned South Coast Children's Society, a highly respected and Christian-run group home system. He was at Orangewood to give me the chance of a lifetime.

He was a saint and will be referred to as such.

The Saint was tall, with a kind smile, and he sauntered over with pure happiness. My confusion must have been evident, as he immediately sat at one of the small tables with stools and patted the empty one for me to come over.

I didn't move.

"Jeremy, this is Bob Ford. He wants you to come live in his group home. Can you believe that?!" the staff member who pointed over to me said.

"Can you come over here?" said one of the male staff members, whom I followed around like a puppy most days. I trusted him, so I jumped up onto the stool and looked into the cool, light brown eyes of the Saint.

"Hey, Jeremy, I am Bob and have heard you have been here quite a long time, right, bud?"

I just nodded, completely confused. I didn't even know the time frame, but it was long enough to see Small Head and a few of the red stars leave to other homes.

"How would you like to come live in my home, where other great kids like you are, and you would be always welcome?" the Saint said easily.

The rest is a bit of a blur, and unfortunately it took a bit longer than expected. The Saint, an amazing human being, actually opened a brand-new group home for me. It might have been a week or two after our first meeting, but I left Hades for good.

Paularino House, in Costa Mesa, was where he wanted me to

live originally, but that plan had a bit of a setback. The poor child who was supposed to leave ended up staying due to his mother or father not having the capacity to care for his emotional needs.

He opened a new home for me. I was the first kid to walk into the Traverse house in Costa Mesa in 1988.

The hazy memories of me leaving the haunted fire bricks of Hades that last time are fleeting. The Saint's excitement and his joy in saving me from such a rough facility were intoxicating. I now had two Bobs rescue me, and I could start seeing my grandfather every weekend again.

CHAPTER 11

TRAVERSE

Costa Mesa, 1988

<hr />

*A house is made with walls and beams; a home is built
with love and dreams.*
—RALPH WALDO EMERSON

The loose taste of freedom was darkly laced with the knowledge of invisible chains on already weak ankles. Lonely kids living in the system know the isolation as a ward of the court, no matter the state they live in. There is a hierarchy, a simple movement upward that many group home children never see and can never truly imagine.

What is this ward of the court hierarchy? Imagine the kingdom is at the top of the mountain, and the slums are at the bottom. Orangewood was the slums, and group homes are one step up from that. The kingdom . . . well, that was adoption.

Orangewood was at the bottom of this level as an orphanage. It was a first or last stop to remove neglected and abused children from homes or the streets. Bottom, in the sense that this is where an institution for helpless children starts so that they can have a better life. Although a scary place for a little child, the alternative is far worse: the streets.

Group homes are a step above. Even with kind staff members, this is not a home but a state-funded organization with fewer kids. Run by a houseparent, staff members, social workers, and psychologists, the group home is meant to provide structure to hurt children.

Immediate shelter homes are next and a taste of what it's like to have a family. They are temporary and used only if nothing else is available, or if Orangewood is full. This construct can lead to foster care, as most of these homes have children living permanently in them.

Foster homes are at the top of this list. Some foster parents want the government paycheck and end up having too many foster kids. It's a horrible situation but still far better than a group home.

A foster home is what group home kids dream of, and there is a long waiting list. One that can become forever, if a child gets too old.

Foster homes have, in most cases, kind, selfless parents and only a few other children. Foster home kids are not labeled as group home kids or orphans at school, and for the most part they have the freedom only one could imagine in a real home. As stated previously, some foster homes have money-hungry parents, and they are what have given that world a bad image.

In some cases, a foster parent knows the state will pay them for a child and exploit this benefit at the cost of innocence. That beautiful four-bedroom home in a great neighborhood has fooled child services, and six unloved foster kids provide a check to the parents. This is a sick truth and happens before they are caught for fraud, neglect, and abuse—but they are caught eventually.

Heartfelt and selfless, Mr. Ford was not someone who put himself first for money. Group home kids receive money from the state, which goes to the maintenance of the home, hiring and keeping staff members, paying for a full-time houseparent, and providing a good quality of life for the poor little children who have been stolen from the life they once had. Vicious cycles of neglect and abuse created a deep-rooted mistrust that even Mr. Ford could not vanquish.

In some very lucky situations, a group home kid is adopted if their parents give up parental rights, but that is a very rare case. Most new parents want a small child, and that is completely understandable. Most of the kids over ten do not expect that to ever happen.

The traverse home saved me. Bob Ford and Bob Butler saved me. God saved me too.

● ● ●

"Hey, Mr. Ford, how far away is the house we are going to?" I asked softly from the back seat of his minivan. It was obvious the vehicle was a means of transport for kids due to all the crumbs and little toys everywhere.

"Jeremy, please call me Bob, like your CASA," he said with a smile while looking at me from the rearview mirror.

"The house is only about twenty minutes away, in Costa Mesa. Do you know where that is?" he asked.

"Nope, is it by Fullerton?" I asked, thinking about living with my mom and Bernie.

"Not far, closer to the beach. Do you like the ocean, Jeremy?"

"I have never been to the ocean," I said softly. A distant memory floated to the surface.

Sounds of the deep blue ocean were a gift in my little ears and created a beautiful harmony with the swaying of palm trees that lined the Pacific Coast Highway. From afar, I could see the triangular gleam of a thousand stars on the ocean, which made me squint. Light rock on the radio was softly built into the memory, and my parents were leaning together in the front seat. I had a couple of G.I. Joes in my hand and had no idea the ocean was so immense.

Cigarette smoke, salty breezes, and my mom's perfume are what the ocean meant to me.

At that point the Saint realized there wasn't much I had done, so he just smiled at me and let me know that everything was going to be okay. I believed him. I trusted him. He was one of the saviors of my life.

My head rolled to the right and woke me up, bumping against the cold window. We arrived at a flat blue house, with a green truck in the front and a heavyset, smiling man in baggy jeans. He was waving at us with both hands, and it was time to meet another hero. Mr. Bill Turner, the first, kindest, and best houseparent.

What is a houseparent?

Child Help, the group home that made me wash my underwear in the toilet, didn't have one, or if they did, I don't remember. Due to the frequency with which hired staff members filtered through group homes, the constant representation of stability falls on the shoulders of the houseparent, who lives in the home as if it were their own.

A houseparent is not always on duty.

Sometimes a houseparent is looking to live for free in a house filled with neglected children simply to offset bills. This is not always the case and should not reflect the true nature of selfless people seeking to help those less fortunate, especially little kids with no families. The houseparent has the responsibility of keeping the home functional. This includes hiring staff members who work around the clock, creating a meal plan with food service, and identifying psychological issues that can be treated by state-approved doctors.

Bill Turner was one of the good ones. I will forever remember his grace toward helping those who were abandoned. Meeting him for the first time was a combination of joy and humor; he made me laugh with his genuine love for life.

"Jeremy!" he shouted in a loud Louisiana drawl that was dusted with a Cajun accent. His hands were outstretched as he walked up to me, hugged me, and picked me up, shaking me slightly in a fatherly way.

There were no words for me; I started tearing up and was immediately embarrassed.

The Cajun and I were attached at the hip. I followed him everywhere from that moment on, until he left a few years later.

The Saint stayed by the car and just smiled until the exchange was over and then said, "Hey, Jeremy, we are all going to a cabin this weekend to go camping. How's that sound?"

Standing by the Cajun's leg, I looked up at him, and he nodded happily. I just smiled and nodded to my Saint, then quickly grabbed Bill's hand, not letting go.

"I will be back in a few hours, Jeremy. I am going to pick up two more boys your age who need a place to live and who will be coming with us camping as well," the Saint said, smiling as he closed the door to the family van.

"How old are you, bud?" the Cajun asked with that intriguing drawl and smile.

"Eight," I said, still holding his hand tightly.

"Oh, great, a few more months and then you will be nine, right?" he said, not letting go of my hand but opening the old screen door to the house. That blue house on Traverse Street would become something I learned to love for many years.

The Cajun guided me into the home, and it was pleasantly quiet. Quiet in a boundless way, like how a library feels. I immediately felt right at home. There was a clean smell to the house that reminded me of cedar and fresh soil, something I would forever connect to that amazing home in Mesa.

To the immediate left, upon walking in, was the dining room, boasting a large wooden table that then led to a galley kitchen, hidden between floating cabinets. Underneath those cabinets was a small counter that had a phone and office supplies splayed along the top.

Behind the homey kitchen was what looked like a door that opened inward to the backyard. Wow . . . a backyard.

Before walking me through the house, we went toward the kitchen, and the Cajun asked if I wanted something to eat. The pantry was near the backyard door, and I was so short it was hard for me to see over the counters in the kitchen, but I said, "Yes."

Poor Bill, though, was not the one who cooked, so he pulled out a few bags of cereal and some milk. I was completely content with that and happy to see the generic brand of Cocoa Puffs—it made the best chocolate milk.

"So, Jeremy, since you're the first kid here, guess what you get to do?" the Cajun asked as he put my empty bowl of Cocoa Puffs in the sink and washed it out.

I just looked up at him inquisitively and shrugged with a smile. He laughed and said, "You can pick your room!"

I stood there, not realizing he was serious. He lightly pushed on my back toward where the rooms were and pointed toward the front door. With the kitchen and dining room to the left, and the living room past that on the same side, the right part of the house had three bedrooms.

Was I in a dream?

I slowly walked past the open front door, feeling a cool ocean breeze float in, and took a right down the dimly lit carpeted hallway. A large closet that had a big combination lock on it was the first door before the bathroom and bedrooms. There were two rooms on the left side and one toward the back on the right past the bathroom.

Both rooms on the left were smaller, so I chose the bigger one on the right. I would stay in that room at the front of the house for years to come.

He sat down on one of the captain-style beds and said calmly, "Do you know what a houseparent is?"

"Um, a parent who stays in the house?" I said, knowing I was being witty.

He just laughed and nodded. "Well, that is just about right, bud, and I am that guy. My room is above the garage on the other side of the dining room, if you ever worry about where I am or need me for anything."

"Okay," I said and sat on the other bed in the room. "When are the other kids getting here?"

"They should be here in a few hours, then we can have some dinner and maybe watch TV. How does that sound?" the Cajun asked.

I nodded happily and looked out one of the two windows in the room, realizing my view was of the nice street we drove up on. There were beautiful homes across the street and people walking around enjoying the warm weather.

"Okay, Jeremy, why don't you relax here for a bit and get situated? Welcome to the Traverse house," the Cajun said, patting my head before walking back to the kitchen area.

All the group homes were named after the streets on which they were built, and I had no idea *Traverse* was even a word.

Waiting for the other kids was hard, and I hoped they were not mean. The Cajun had turned on the TV in the living room, and I could hear him laughing at something, but since he told me to relax, I stayed in the room—my room. Hearing a car, I looked out the window, seeing Bob's minivan pull in, and it was just enough for me to run out and tell Bill.

The Cajun waited outside for them too.

Johnny Pierson and Peter Armet arrived as I had to Traverse. The Saint walked in with them as they excitedly ran to the kitchen, where Cajun brought them. The Saint had a couple of bags of what looked like Chinese food, and it smelled delicious.

Both the boys smiled at me, which was a good sign they would not bully me. They were pretty big kids too. Johnny said, "Hey, ever had orange chicken, dude?"

I shook my head with big eyes and a bigger stomach.

Johnny smiled and punched my shoulder gently and said in an excited voice, "It is the best thing you will ever eat!"

Peter was looking intently at the bags of orange chicken, and his mouth was partially open in a starving way. He was developmentally disabled and had a brain shunt in the side of his head near his right temple. We all immediately got along.

Peter towered over me and probably weighed one hundred pounds more than I did, but I felt responsible for him in the home since I was the first kid. He was half Mexican and some other ethnicity but took after his Latino side, with dark hair, dark almond eyes, and light brown skin.

He had the choice of his room but wanted to be my roommate.

"Um, can I, uh, be in the same room as you, Jeremy?" he asked me shyly.

We sat at the table eating mouthwatering orange chicken and Chinese noodles that I had never seen before, but they were delicious. Chicken lo mein and orange chicken became my favorite Chinese food for years after that.

"Yeah!" I said excitedly. He was a kind, big kid who very much needed a friend, and I did too.

Johnny had already staked out his room, across from mine, which also looked out on the street, and he was not upset at all that Peter wanted to bunk with me. Johnny had this coolness about him that made me want to do everything he did. He was tall, but not even close to how giant Peter was. His hair was sandy blond, and he kept it long, like a surfer covering his eyes.

As we sat and ate like savages, everything felt good, and I could not believe Orangewood was a distant memory. My always wandering mind dreamed of weekends with my grandpa.

It seemed like there was someone out there looking out for me and keeping me safe. Keeping me from more pain and hurt. Things could have worked out a lot worse for me, and I was going to make sure I was the best kid possible.

My mother was just a figment of my imagination, and her silence weighed heavily on me. The feeling of not being wanted sank into the very core of my being. This time a rescue twinkled beside me and through me.

The next day came quickly, and we could not wait to go camping. Not sure if it was a Friday or Saturday, but it was a weekend.

"So, who is ready to go camping?" the Saint asked as he walked in with Winchell's Donuts. I knew that logo, as my grandpa took me there most Saturdays.

All of us, including the Cajun, said, "I am!"

We were so excited that Peter and I ran into each other hard, and I went flying into a wall. He picked me up easily and was laughing in a way that felt so genuine I laughed too. Although he was older, his mind was much younger, and it made him who he was.

There was not much for us to bring, and Bob said he had

everything we needed at the cabin up in Big Bear, about three hours from Costa Mesa. Camping brought back memories of Donna, from the immediate shelter home, and how she gave me love when there was none to give. I missed her and her cooking.

"Okay, boys, let's get in the van and start moving so we can be there by dark," the Saint said. The winking sun above was already sailing from its high point, and the shadows were stretching across the ground in a responsive dance.

"Who wants to get a fire going and have s'mores?" the Saint said.

We all did a happy dance while jumping in the van.

I think us boys felt the immediate shock of kindness in a mean world that took our innocence too early, and all three of us just smiled. The Saint and Cajun knew what we were emotionally going through and gently closed the door to the van so we could head out. They gave us puffy Cheetos to snack on and bottled waters.

I felt as if I were driving away from my home on vacation, not a place that infected joy with pain and destroyed happiness with isolation. Peter and I sat together in the middle row while Johnny took up the back row, smacking the back of our heads playfully.

We were already inseparable, and I had never felt this free.

CHAPTER 12

MOUNTAINS

Big Bear, 1988

It is not the mountain we conquer, but ourselves.
—SIR EDMUND HILLARY

Mighty pine trees shot into the heavens as we strained our little necks against the windows inside the van to look for the green canopies above. There was instrumental blues music in the background that reflected the Cajun's culture, and he lounged in the front seat, moving his head from side to side, humming. The Saint, with his left hand gently resting over the wheel and his gold watch shining brightly, was cruising up the mountain with ease.

Green blurs from the archaic trees blended smoothly with the rough grays, ambers, and browns of the huge granite boulders lining the road. There was bedrock everywhere, and yellow signs that warned of falling rocks lined the highway every few miles. Quite a few cars were moving up the winding mountain roads toward Big Bear, and the excitement grew with each passing expansive turn.

"How are you boys doing back there?" the Cajun hollered happily.

All at different times, we yelled back, "Awesome! Great! Amazing!" This new life was surreal; I couldn't believe everything had changed so significantly and so quickly.

Energy was in the air and sizzled all around us. We could not escape the purity of oxygen as we left the ocean-scented cities behind and drove into what was the most beautiful place on earth.

Shadows transformed into long, gloomy creatures along the roads and up the unshaded mountain face as the setting sun turned the Southern California sky a deep amethyst. The pillowed clouds stretched into light pink streamers of translucent animal shapes that faded out toward the sparkling Pacific Ocean horizon and became a part of the beautiful sunset.

Mystified by the changing colors of the sky, I lost myself in the drive up the coniferous-coated mountain and the new feeling of belonging. This luxurious feeling gave me goose bumps and shivers, thinking of freedom. A few days ago, I was getting ready for bed, in a white cell within the old brick walls of Orangewood.

The comfort of driving, the clean, cool air billowing in from the open windows, and the mesmerizing landscape cascading by created a recipe for magnificent sleep. The other boys must have nodded off. Silence ensued.

I let the feeling guide me toward a wonderful land of perfect sleep.

Soft braking and the sound of gravel under tires gently woke us up.

"Okay, boys, we are here!" said a sleepy Saint.

The Cajun opened the sliding doors, and our adventure began.

The first thing I noticed was the darkness. It was complete. It brought out fear.

Dark came at me from everywhere, until I looked up and saw the most breathtaking sky of glittering stars imaginable. The other boys saw me looking up, and we all just stood there with staggering awe.

We felt ourselves slowly drawn toward the cabin, but it was impossible to not stare straight up. The tips of the large pine trees way above shone like perfect beacons, and the deep rustling of the needles was something we could feel as much as hear. There was no color, and everything was black or gray, with the sounds of the forest slowly coming back to life.

There was no sound besides our movement, and the forest was alive with existence.

Our feet crunching on the gravel driveway was loud and overwhelmed the new world. No light came from the cabin, but the half-moon bathed the front porch in a symbolic welcome. That moon was looking at us and pointed its brilliance right at the front porch.

"Watch your step, boys, and wait out front with Bill until I can turn on the lights. We don't need to go right to the hospital," said the always enthusiastic Saint.

Everyone heard the Saint find the light switch, and that silence evaporated.

Once the lights took away those dark, shadowy tentacles, a beautifully decorated cabin awaited. It was from a painting or a movie, and I could not believe we would get to sleep there.

All of us boys tiptoed in and stayed by the door, not knowing what to do. The Cajun had already walked to the kitchen and turned on some lights.

There we saw nice wooden bunks in one room that we all got to pick. Since I was the smallest, I took the top bunk of one, while the other boys had the bottom ones. Everyone was tired, but that sleepiness quickly went away once we saw the snacks.

The Saint brought out around the table a couple of boxes of this popcorn called Crunch 'n Munch, which none of us had ever heard of but all of us loved. The Cajun ate a few pieces, but mostly just watched us enjoy ourselves as he spoke quietly with the Saint.

The drive took a bit longer, so we stayed inside with a wood fire blazing and watched TV. Our awesome hosts were in another room, laughing and leaving us alone, but would come in occasionally to warm up against the hearth.

After a while, the perfect warmth of the fire had our heads falling to our chests on those soft couches.

They told us to go up the beautiful log stairs that shone with a lacquered glow to brush our teeth and shower. "We are going to have pancakes for breakfast!" Bob yelled up to us as we all got ready. I could not remember ever actually having homemade pancakes before, but I didn't want anyone to know that.

We all slept peacefully that night. My bunk was near the window, and I could see the half-moon watching over me. Everything was pitch black, and that night sky was the last thing I remembered before the sandman took me.

I was lying on the top bunk, watching bright morning rays of light escaping through the dusty blinds and listening to the overpowering snoring that Peter somehow managed to emit, thinking to myself this was still a dream. How could this truly be real?

I had been awake for a while, just staring out into the forest. I had never seen anything so beautiful.

Soft clanging downstairs was my motivator to sneak down and peek through the railings toward the kitchen. The Saint was awake, fully dressed in an apron, humming to himself as he prepared the ingredients to what would be the best flapjacks I ever had. He turned around and looked right at me.

"Hey, buddy, want to help?" he whispered.

I had to control my running so he would not know how excited I was. My hug onto his leg quickly gave that away. He was an angel who lived on being selfless and kind. His approach to life was what centered and created the moral compass by which I lived my life.

"Have you had flapjacks before?" he asked me as he moved his spatula quickly. "These are from my family recipe, and you will love them."

I was not sure at that point if it was a question or not.

"I have had pancakes before. Are they the same thing?" I asked, seeing the box he used to get the batter going.

"That is correct. We call them flapjacks in Louisiana," the Saint said, smiling.

As the bright morning progressed, the Cajun and the other boys came down to eat delicious flapjacks with real maple syrup— another amazing thing I had never had before. Time blended that day, and we lounged around, enjoying the serenity.

The Saint let us wander around the cabin but asked us all to stay together. We climbed trees, chased small animals, and made a fort out of branches. We were within earshot of the cabin and played around our tree castle for hours.

We heard the Cajun yell for us, and we came scampering back with hair full of pine needles, dirty hands, and huge smiles.

Time to sit by the fire out back of the cabin and have the long-awaited s'mores. I had never seen anyone build a fire, and the light in the sky was still bright enough to be considered dusk.

Whispers of gray ash floated up toward the everlasting darkness and hovered near the swirling flames. Hearing the crackling of the wood while silence pushed toward us felt wonderful. No one spoke while ash rained down, and we all felt the calmness take over—a heavy blanket covering pain.

I could see the other boys across the fire, but behind them was complete blackness. The feeling of being watched magnified as the sounds of the forest came alive, and our imaginations ran rampant. Every twig snap or animal sound way up in the invisible trees became a bear or mountain lion. We huddled closer to the warmth, waiting for a turn with marshmallows.

The Cajun demonstrated the art of keeping a flame alive on an innocent marshmallow and to burn it just right so that it melted but didn't turn to black tar. The trick was slowly rotating the stick, holding the gooey substance until it had just the right amount of char.

My first marshmallow fell in the fire.

My second burned so bad we had to throw the stick away. I got the third to squish between two golden crackers and melting chocolate pieces inside. Most of it got on my face, but it was supposed to. We had the euphoric face of food bliss all night.

We were in heaven and never wanted that weekend to end. Elementary school loomed in the distance, and I had never been to a public school for more than a few weeks at a time.

The fear of learning how to read, write, and do math stemmed from embarrassment. Most eight-year-old kids were far beyond my abilities, and it was going to show.

The next day we drove back down toward the ocean and what was to be a new adventure.

●●●

Peter snored loudly.

His breathing was that of an elephant with a cold, and no number of pillows over my head could stem the constant outpouring of honking from the bed next to me. The first night back at the Traverse home my stomach was queasy from nervous thoughts. We had school the next morning, and I needed to find somewhere to sleep. I quickly moved to the empty room, blanket roll in hand, and truly felt bad for Peter, but it was the only way.

Metal clanging woke me out of a deep slumber, in a foreign place, and gave me instant fear before I realized I was in the group home, not somewhere isolated in Orangewood. It was quiet, other than what was going on in the kitchen, and early morning light shown through old curtains that looked like they were made of thin, curved metal.

The smell of bacon quickly pulled me toward the kitchen, like freshly baked pie on a windowsill in *Tom and Jerry*. Floating toward the lip-smacking smells fueled by the rumbling in my empty tummy, I was lost in the moment of hunger.

"You must be Jeremy!" A sweet elderly female voice took over my thoughts as I peeked into the kitchen.

"Uh, hey," I whispered with a bit of a hoarse morning voice.

"Would you like some eggs and bacon?" she continued sweetly, and she didn't wait for a response. Her motions were swift, and she had an aura of kindness.

Who was this nice lady?

She patted the seat close to where Bill's door was, to his suite upstairs over the garage, and said, "Here you go! Eat up!"

I remember feeling immediately at home and instantly connected to her. The fluffy eggs and crispy bacon were just icing on this already amazing cake of life.

Her name was Alice, and she wore a moo-moo grandma dress. She was a sweet elderly lady who believed garlic pills helped everything in life and owned a consignment shop not too far away. She was the first staff member at the Traverse home and was in charge of getting the kids ready in the morning.

She knew I was scared of going to school and sat next to me with her hand on my quivering shoulder without saying much other than, "You can do this. I believe in you."

I had never been on a school bus, and neither had Peter nor Johnny. Yet here we were, with Moo-Moo, waiting on a bus to come to ship us off to school right up the street from our house, about five houses away. The fear was overwhelming, and I felt my body shaking.

Sonora Elementary School, in Costa Mesa, was my first taste of academic anxiety. It made my stomach problems worse and formed a dark dread at dealing with "normal" kids. It was impossible to hide who I was, where I came from or lived, and I would quickly become the kid who was easy to make fun of.

Just yesterday, I had been enjoying that tranquil life in the San Bernardino Mountains with two of my group home buddies and dreaming of what life would be like outside the confines of loneliness brought on by Orangewood.

Not realizing how merciless and terrible kids could be, I enthusiastically went to my third-grade homeroom class with Mrs. Walters. It was immediately obvious every little kid knew each other; they had their groups, and nobody cared who I was.

Even being walked in by the principal himself and a warm welcome from the teacher left me scared. I ended up sitting next to a Vietnamese boy named Lan Pham, who smiled at me but turned his shoulder so I couldn't see what was on his paper.

There was no way I was pooping in the school bathroom, and holding it all day was going to be excruciating. Mrs. Walters didn't know my problems with going to the bathroom, and I was not telling anyone. I felt like I smelled or something since different kids kept staring at me in disgust.

"Jeremy, please turn in your multiplication work. You are the last one left," the teacher said pointedly, and I looked down at an empty piece of paper. I had never done math, and I didn't understand the numbers on the chalkboard. I felt like crying and was pretty sure there were tears in my eyes as the snickering of kids around me made it obvious I was the center of the jokes.

"Okay, Mrs. Walters," I said softly, walking up to her with the blank paper.

She saw the fear on my face and the blank paper, then said nothing as she squeezed my shoulder in understanding. Mrs. Walters knew right away what had happened and asked me to stay as the other kids went to recess.

"You don't know what I am teaching, right, Jeremy?" she asked softly and innocently.

I felt like trusting her, and I was by nature a very trusting person and responded with, "I have never done math before, Mrs. Walters."

"Well, we are going to fix that!" She smiled and handed me a big folder of papers.

"What is this?" I asked, holding the heavy binder.

"This is what you will be studying at home. Don't worry—nobody will make fun of you," she responded.

CHAPTER 13

WARD

Costa Mesa, 1989

———————

A recipe has no soul. You, as the cook, must bring soul to the recipe.
—THOMAS KELLER

An underlying fog of doubt, dark and ominous, swept through my mind, covering every corner. With it came insecurity, anxiousness, fear, and loneliness. I wore a veil of bravado emitting denial, anger, and panic. The loss of everything was hard to bear, and I hid behind a happy smile.

●●●

His light shone from far away, and when it came closer to me, the shadows of loneliness evaporated. I knew Grandpa's visits were just the eye in the storm of my life, but he was able to steer me clear of unforgiving wreckage.

Time was a gift my grandpa blessed me with every weekend. He was always there, never late, and the most consistent person in my life. I was beyond lucky to have been given this gift of time and never once took it for granted.

Grandpa, his presence alone, was protective and kind, yet with an underlying sense of purpose. He made sure to meet the group home staff and speak to all of them before driving me away. I never asked him what the conversations were about.

Every drive away from the group home to his lagoon house in Huntington Beach was a blessing. Even the sun on my face felt different when I was with my grandpa and his family. I felt free, and when we got close to his home, I felt raw excitement.

At my grandpa's, the food was always amazing, and Bella cooked from her heart. It was a taste-bud explosion, coming from the bland meals at the home. I was never hungry, though, and that was a gift from God. I knew kids who didn't eat, besides breakfast and lunch at school. No snacks, no nice drinks, and no money.

Of all the morning staff, Moo-Moo stayed, and she was the sweetest old lady. Some mornings she would talk to us about vitamins, healthy living, and promised to take us to her consignment shop so we could go next door and paint pottery.

Mama Reata, who was there on weekends and some weekdays, saved me too. Nobody had ever been as kind and loving to me as Reata. I had forgotten what motherly love felt like. She was an artist and creative at heart; she brought out my inner drawer.

She was a beautiful Black woman who quickly saw my love for drawing and coloring. I craved her approval and spent hours every day drawing. I filled page upon page of whatever thing entered my mind, and Mama Reata would look at every one, providing tips that taught me.

"Draw lightly here so you can erase it cleaning after," Mama

Reata told me when I was sketching out a cartoon figure.

"Make sure to be gentle—the pencil can break easily," she told me a few times when I pushed too hard with colored pencils.

It was a true apprenticeship in the art of a creative lifeforce. Our spirits were similar, and I felt the same energy. There was no way I was anything other than a creative person, and it was something I would work hard at.

I know Mama Reata spent her own money to get me nice drawing paper, colored pencils, fine-tipped markers, and stencils. She was happy to do it and loved teaching me art, but I made sure to pay her back with well-thought-out drawings.

In the early days, Traverse was a very well-oiled machine, and things were good.

We had nighttime staff members who would arrive as we got ready for bed. Their focus was to make sure we stayed in our rooms, didn't run away, or steal anything from the kitchen. They were also in charge of administering evening medication, as needed, and keeping that closet locked up tight.

Many of those kids were kleptomaniacs and loved to steal.

The Cajun was always around and available. His caring came from deep within his soul.

He told me all the time, "You are such a smart and loving young man, Jeremy. I just know God has plans for you!"

The Cajun would sneak up and tickle me, pick me up, and throw me on the couch. In the mornings, he would help Moo-Moo with breakfast and getting us rambunctious kids out the door.

One of the staff members, Walter, was fun and like a big brother. He picked us up and ran around with tremendous speed.

Even when he was winded, he made sure all the little kids got a turn. I called him Flash.

I am not sure if Mama Reata and Flash got along, but they worked together quite a bit.

Flash helped me get over my bowel trouble. Not sure why, but he really made sure to support me and even worked with the therapists as a team. It was like a weight of paranoia, embarrassment, and disgust was lifted from an insidious perch on which those awful feelings sat, mocking me.

Flash would frequently say, "Always keep your head up; always fight for it."

I did and never had a stomach issue again.

Patty and Michelle were supersweet young women, both attending California State University, Fullerton. As part of their clinical master's program, they began working at group homes. They poured out love and affection to all the kids, even when it was not reciprocated. They got tons of childish love from me, as I could never get enough hugs, touches, or cuddles.

"Jeremy, God has blessed you with such a big heart, and this is his book, made just for you," Patty said to me after handing me a beautiful NIV Bible made for young adults, with a personal bookmark in the shape of a *J*.

Orangewood no longer lurked in the background of my life. Nobody knew where my mother was, and it was probably for the best. Bernie and Aunt Sherrie disappeared. My dad's side of the family never once came to see if I was alive.

Due to my attachment with Mama Reata, I felt bad leaving to see my grandpa on the weekends. I didn't want the other kids to get time with her instead of me. This was purely out of selfishness and the first real feeling of jealousy.

When I did go see Grandpa, Mama Reata would leave me beautiful letters that used shapes in place of many of the words. Her love was something I cherished and tightly held on to.

Reata would tell me every day, "Jeremy, I just love you so much it hurts!" Then squeeze me in a huge hug.

● ● ●

School mornings were hectic, tumultuous, and a bit stressful if we didn't follow the routine. Moo-Moo got to the home at 6:00 a.m., and if we were smart, we would listen for her car. This way I would not get ready late or get negative marks on the Traverse score chart.

The score chart—what a wonderful tool for those who wanted to do well.

"Jeremy, gold star for completing all your daily tasks," a staff member would say.

This star, this amazing token, was a daily reminder to do the right thing. It felt good and right when I had a responsibility or was asked to do something. I did it without questioning or fighting back.

I tried to do the right things at school too. That didn't stop the bullying or the taunting.

I was always an easy target. Knowing they were coming, and there was nothing I could do about it, made me fearful every day. How sad it was to prefer the confines of a group home rather than face the torment at school.

It started with a punch to the head or getting stuffed between the seats of the bus. They would open up my backpack and throw all my stuff on top of me, laughing hysterically. The other group home kids were smart to not intervene—the target was on me.

"Kick him, spit on him, and slap his head!" they would yell, until the bus driver intervened too late.

It was on one of these days a cholo named Junior, who was in sixth grade, living on another street down from ours, got on the bus and sat behind me with a look of menace. His older brothers were part of some sect of the Mexican Mafia in Orange County, and he was proud to be from a gangster family. So proud that he sought out ways to fight anyone, even older kids in high school, and I was the unfortunate one to be sitting in front of him.

There was a sense of trepidation that made the air on the bus thick with silence, and I couldn't wait to just get out of there. By the time we got to Sonora Elementary, I thought I was safe and rushed to get off the bus. That was a mistake.

He was behind me, and I could feel his rage.

He kicked me off the bus hard as I was trying to get down the stairs, and I landed on the side of my head. "You little bitch. Nobody likes you," Junior whispered as he kicked me in the side and ran off.

It was a bad fall, and he knew it. I slowly lifted myself up, but Junior was long gone. This was the way of things then, and the bus driver kept going. Other kids walked past, but not before saying something and laughing.

Nebulous thoughts bubbled up in my dizzy head as I got up and tried to hurry into class before the morning bell rang. I would not tell anyone anything. Mrs. Walters saw me and immediately made a loud gasp, all the while pulling me outside the classroom.

"Jeremy, your face is bloody!" she whispered loudly and rushed me to the nurse.

When I hit the pavement, my right cheekbone must have slid a bit along the rough ground. It was a messy gash with sticky blood that I didn't know was there. My right elbow was also scratched and bleeding.

"The nurse will clean you up, and when you are ready, you can come back to class. We are going to have to call the home though, Jeremy," Mrs. Walters said tragically.

She knew what that meant. She knew Junior, even though she didn't know him, would find out someone told on him, and he would blame me. His gangster family would as well.

"No, please don't! Please don't call!" I begged uselessly.

The kind nurse looked at me and smiled sadly. "Let's get you all cleaned up, big boy, and call over the principal. He is going to need you to give a statement."

I said, "I slipped off the bus."

Big, inflamed cuts on the side of my face and my arm were red banners for kids to make fun of me. The group home kid who got beat up by Junior.

The group home kid who kept his mouth shut.

He left me alone after that, and I never said who did it, even though the Cajun tried to softly interrogate me. I was in third grade and got beat down by a sixth grader, who had older gangster brothers who lived close by. The Cajun knew the deal, and although he tried to get me to talk, he respected my silence.

I never said a word about the incident, and gangster Junior knew it because he was still at the school.

I knew where he hung out with his thug homies—by the blue monkey bars—and stayed far away. Being small, it was easy to hide, and I sneaked around near where the Vietnamese kids played card games under the shade of the classroom buildings.

They never bothered me and left me alone to watch them play a game called thirteen, which was essentially poker with the whole deck. The rules were different, and sometimes they would teach me the game or share their broken-up ramen packs.

Junior and his crew left me alone after that, and I stayed clear of where they hung out. He knew I never told, and for that he didn't beat me up anymore.

CHAPTER 14

CHAINS

Costa Mesa, 1989–1990

─────

When you're nice, you're not bullying people. But when you're kind,
you stand up against the bully.
—DANIEL LUBETZKY

Getting through a day at Sonora Elementary without finding the fist or foot of a bully required precision. I began to figure out who they were, where they liked to hang out, and more importantly, the locations they used to beat up their victims. Most of this intel stemmed from getting pushed around and spat on every single day.

Mrs. Walters and the fifth-grade math teacher, Mr. Wotta, who was also the basketball coach, looked out for me. They could not be everywhere at once. Coach was protective of the underdogs, and I was just that. He would make sure to bring me into basketball scrimmages at recess, to keep an eye on me, and walked me back to class.

Coach valued my intelligence and saw very quickly I had a way with words. I went from barely understandable sentences to perfect in-between-the-line writing. There was something that made me feel good about writing, and I enjoyed seeing words come together on paper.

"Good job, bud! You have come a long way!" Coach would say. Sometimes he sat down with me at a picnic bench so that I was not alone. He knew I was getting bullied.

The problem was getting on the bus.

It was like a gauntlet of terror, and there was no way around it. Around one corner, a kid would trip me and then kick me or grab my backpack to throw me into a wall. Other times I got spit on or gum thrown at me. Someone was constantly calling me something derogatory.

Other group home kids got it, too, but I was the only one who was not associated with some clique. Peter was in the special education area of Sonora and even took a different bus home, so we never saw each other at school. Johnny was in sixth grade, but he was popular and in a clique.

By the time I made it on the bus, I felt safer. Junior and the other gangster kids liked to walk home or mess around at the school after class. This was an everyday thing—a sick adventure that created distress. An hour before school ended, the fear would set in, and sometimes I would run to the bus just to avoid confrontation.

Reata would be waiting at the bus stop for me, or it would be Patty and Michelle.

In the early days of the Traverse home, Mama Reata was there a lot during the week. As she started her professional development, her time at the home was centered more on the weekends. This meant I would not see her as much, unless I didn't see my grandpa.

There was safety in the group home, and I had been given more than most of the kids I met at Orangewood. It was not every day my body was thrown in front of the bully bulldozer, and on many occasions the school was pretty awesome.

Walking through the doors of the Traverse house didn't feel like home, but it felt right. I belonged and had clean clothes and hot food that came with a comfy bed that was not in a cell. We were supposed to do homework when we got off the bus, but most kids just lied so they could watch TV or hang out in their rooms. Many of the boys had relatives who brought them things they could enjoy.

I did my homework and enjoyed hanging out in the dining room with the staff members. They answered all my ridiculous questions and gave me the attention I craved every day. We were given snacks and drinks when we got home from school. Those little things mattered.

Our long street was the last one in a line of urban homes, and behind our house was the 405 freeway. There was a huge tope sound wall one could see from our backyard, and it didn't block the car engines that well. The fence that surrounded our home was meant to keep us in, not out.

We were monitored in the backyard too.

Group home kids were not allowed to be unsupervised. Many times, we would ask to go outside but could not if the staff members were busy dealing with other kids. It was understandable, as some of the angry ones would act violently toward anyone within range.

The thought of having to ask to hang out in our backyard was annoying, but it also made us not want to go anywhere. On occasion, we would go as a group to the nearby park to shoot hoops, throw footballs or Frisbees, and the Saint would come by with food. That was fun and got us out of the house, but it was rare during the weekdays.

That local park had a beautifully maintained grass field that always seemed to have a glossy layer of dew on it, no matter the time of day. It was at least two football fields side by side and had a full-size basketball court in the back-right corner. In the front, right by the parking lot, two wood gazebos sat at right angles from each other and had red picnic tables underneath.

We could walk, but there were no shortcuts through the neighborhood. We would drive most of the time, and that field was usually empty. The park was open all around, with no fences, and had two entrances from the street, with one exiting out to the main road, Paularino Street.

It was also home to teenage thugs who enjoyed hassling anyone who got near their pickup basketball games or if they had taken over the gazebos. They would even threaten the group home staff and would wait for the cops to show up before they ran off, messing up our day and sometimes yelling at us in jest.

Many of the kids had problems relaxing at home, and they always needed something to do or someone to bother. I, on the other hand, could hang out and chill all day with no problem. Staying out of trouble with those kids was another story.

A couple of days a week, the staff members and the shrinks would coordinate a therapy session, and it was miserable.

"Okay, boys, let's all meet up in the living room to talk to the psychologist," a staff member would yell back toward the rooms.

Shiplap had nothing on the crazy wood walls in that dark living room. The paneling, or whatever it was, had three or four different brown colors that angled in directions that had no cohesive pattern. There were floor lamps that projected a yellow hue onto the wooden wall and a squeaky frosted-glass ceiling fan that always had a thick layer of dust on it.

Our main source of light in the living room was a long sliding-glass door that was framed along the back of the house. Sometimes the Cajun would light a fire in the old brick fireplace, which was missing more pieces than it had.

This was where we would have mandatory therapy sessions.

Chairs from the kitchen were brought in to form an awkward circle, with the psychologist sitting nearest the exit. These wood chairs added to the dark ship theme and had orange flower-pattern cushions. It was dreadful knowing we had to sit there for an hour twice a week.

Even with all this negative interaction with other kids, I enjoyed talking with everyone, especially the therapists. They were not there to make life hard and genuinely cared about the kids' well-being.

I made sure to be the first one in so I could sit right across from the therapist. I craved attention, and they never had to worry about me.

"Mr. Jeremy, always early!" said Sandy Kates, our first therapist. He was not a clinical psychologist but a certified social worker and pediatric therapist.

His salt-and-pepper beard was short and blended into a gray-haired ponytail. Sandy had deep smile wrinkles down the outside of his eyes, although he could have only been in his early fifties. He smoked a lot of cigarettes and hid the smell with cologne. I called him Smokey.

Smokey was the king of flannel shirts, and I had never seen him with the same one. Birkenstocks with socks and baggy jeans that looked like they had been washed so many times they probably couldn't take another spin cycle were his getup.

"Hey, Sandy! Nice flannel!" I would say every time, which became a joke that made his smile wrinkles more prominent.

"Can I have that one? I like the light blue," I asked.

"I don't think so, buddy. Where are all the other kids?" he asked genuinely.

"Patty and Michelle are getting them," I said. They didn't have a single bad bone in their bodies.

With all the kids sitting around the chairs, and Smokey saying hi to all of them, we got started on what normally would be an uncomfortable situation.

Negative attitudes were passed around like a peace pipe, and the boys acted as if they were sitting in purgatory's waiting room. Hands fidgeted, eyes were downcast, and all the answers were one or two words. Awkward silences pushed past the kindness that emanated from Sandy, and he was a true professional by not letting that darkness infect him.

The other boys thought I was a bit of a suck-up; I loved to talk and answer questions. I didn't care at all, and I probably was. What I enjoyed most was trying to help the staff feel less guilty and fill the void of silence that was created through the other kids' negative attitudes.

Diving into the deepest part of a child's heart was not the purpose of the meetings. It was a wellness check and to see how we were fitting in. This included school and other activities we were a part of, such as going out on weekends with family.

I loved talking about my grandpa, as he was my only tie to the outside world. The Saint would come to the sessions and take a few of us out for hamburgers or tacos, but that was not as often as when he first opened the home. His success with helping children and building a booming business left little time for what was.

Smokey spoke of how we could be good young men, and he encouraged us to take the right path, when it came to making decisions. He was always an advocate for us and would use his own money to buy us things we needed.

South Coast Children's Society invested in their people and children. We were given money to get school clothes, and we went on outings. The staff members were always caring and made sure to make us feel loved as best they could in the time they had.

After the group sessions, many of the kids felt overwhelmed and would go to their rooms to hide out. If enough kids wanted to go to the backyard, we would throw footballs or bask in the late afternoon sun. With enough practice, I could pretend it was not a group home.

Bedtime was early, around eight thirty, and I was okay with that, as it got me closer to seeing my grandpa on the weekends. He was what gave me hope every single week.

The days and weeks at the Traverse home blended rapidly.

Boys came in and left rather quickly, sometimes within a month, but I was always there. When I would ask about my mother, the Saint and Smokey would say encouraging things. "Jeremy, your mother is doing better and in a halfway house," the Saint said on one occasion.

"What is a halfway house?" I asked, intrigued.

The Saint squeezed my hand and said, "It's like a group home for adults to help them."

That made sense to me, so I asked, "Will she come see me soon, or can I live with her?"

His face was pained when he answered, and I knew it was hard on him. "We hope so, Jeremy. We hope so."

He left it at that, and I could tell he didn't want to get my hopes up.

Kids in the home received calls almost daily, and family would visit during the week as well as on weekends. Having my grandpa take me away from Traverse allowed me to forget group home life for a few days, but I remember seeing some of the boys who didn't have a place to go look out their bedroom windows at me.

I asked once, "Can we bring one of the other kids from the group home, Grandpa?"

We were driving in his Ranger, and he took a moment to answer. It was so long I thought I had angered him. He never got angry or annoyed, so the memory was vivid.

"I wish we could, Jeremy, but I am only allowed to be your CASA, and it's very selfless of you to ask that," he eventually said without looking at me.

In his truck, I would sit as close to him as possible on the tan bucket seats, but not too close, or he would have trouble shifting gears. I would play with the hair on his arm and ask him questions nonstop, but the closeness we shared was what saved me from so many wrong paths.

The feeling of leaving the group home was unexplainable. I would be anxious all night Friday, waiting for my grandpa to come pick me up early Saturday. We had our routine, and I never realized how important that was, until much later in life. He gave me hope, and even with my mother not in the picture, he was always positive about me seeing her again.

"I bet you, Jeremy, she is doing well in the halfway house just so she can see you again," the Saint would say emphatically.

I believed him. But that was not the case.

WE CANNOT PROCESS YOUR ORDER
IF THE PROOFS ARE REMOVED!!

POSE I

PKG. A ☐ F ☐
B ☐ G ☐
C ☐ H ☐
D ☐ J ☐
E ☐

POSE II

PKG. B ☐ F ☐
C ☐ G ☐
D ☐ H ☐
E ☐ J ☐

CHAPTER 15

ANNANDALE

Idyllwild, California, 1990

—————

Sorrow is a fruit. God does not make it grow on limbs
too weak to bear it.
—VICTOR HUGO

Low, rolling fog covered the ground where two big yellow buses slowly rumbled. It was so early the sun had not crested its horizon, but tiny rays of light broke through the deep darkness of night. The only sounds came from the dew-covered buses and kids forming up by their last name to get on their specific transport.

Effervescent emotions rolled through me at the Annandale pickup site that morning. The Cajun dropped Johnny and me off, walking us toward the gathering of people. Johnny ran straight to someone he knew, leaving me in the dust. I didn't know anyone and felt a bit nervous.

"Hey, champ, you doing okay?" I heard someone say behind me with a soft Hispanic accent.

Turning around, a heavyset Latino man wearing a

red-and-green camp counselor sweatshirt on was smiling at me. It was infectious, and I smiled back immediately.

"You know where you are going?" he asked.

"Jeremy," I said, still smiling.

I looked back toward the Cajun's truck, and he waved to me. He was a caring guy, and I would miss him for this week at summer camp. Camp Annandale was a Christian camp that was tailored toward children in need and in the system.

"Everyone calls me JerBear," he said enthusiastically and picked up my things to put under the bus.

"Can I get on?" I asked softly.

"Of course, champ. We are leaving in about fifteen minutes and going to have the time of your life at camp!" he said, doing little jig while walking me up to the bus.

The driver had a happy-go-lucky attitude, with a kind face and mustache, and everyone called him Pretzel.

"Hey there! Get on up and find a seat, but remember: the back is the bumpiest!" Pretzel said.

I went to the back after giving him a high five and smile. "Okay!" I said quickly.

Looking around at the other kids, they also looked a bit frightened. Others had done this before and were all open to sitting next to me. I could hide a bit in the very back and look out the rear door windows.

Two pretty Hispanic girls were in the back-left seats, sitting together, so I jumped into the right pleather seat with an open smile. It was always easier for me to make friends with girls, and I knew this was going to be a fun trip. I waved and said, "Hi."

I recognized another group home kid from the Paularino house who came to sit next to me. He was the same age as me and small as well.

South Coast Children's Society had seven different group homes by the time I was nine, and the Paularino Street house was one for kids around the same age as Traverse, with similar emotional issues. He was a quiet red-headed kid who liked to read and wanted to sit by the window. I was fine with that; I could talk to the nice girls next to me.

The bus driver made sure we were all sitting down before introducing himself as Pretzel. JerBear and a few other counselors were scattered around the bus. All around me kids were whispering, talking, or giggling, and there was a sense of happiness.

We sang along to Christian songs I had never heard before, and the staff told stories that enthralled us all into silence. Time stood still, and the gentle driving of the bus took me to la-la land.

Tender silence took over with whispers from the counselors, who had moved up to the front to talk with the bus driver. Most of the kids had been rocked to sleep with the morning light still low in the awakening sky.

The scenery was cosmically surreal. Looking down at the energy-vibing mountain, I saw the expanding sun marking everything in its glorious path, burning out the shadows.

We were so high up it seemed like the light gray clouds were made of cotton balls and could be plucked out of the sky. A long dark tunnel with yellow lights was carved into the mountainside. It was the entrance into a whole new world.

The other side was another time in space—to a haven of perfect trees and life. It was not long before everyone became restless, knowing we were approaching the camp.

It was magical. It was freedom. It was belonging.

The air was so clean I could feel the oxygen around us. Perfect pine needles fell off the trees like green-tinted snow. The canopies blocked out most of the sun, and there were early morning shadows everywhere. Birds and insects echoed everywhere, with creatures scurrying in the hidden brush. It was breathtaking.

A beautiful two-story wooden cabin with a two-story deck emerged from the trees as the bus drove toward the gravel parking area. More colorful counselors waited for us happily with waving arms. It felt like a dream, and I could not believe group home kids got this type of attention.

A big outdoor pool to the right of the property was glimmering, and huge granite boulders were everywhere the eye could see. Happy kids couldn't wait to get off the bus. It had been a long drive but was just a couple of hours into the San Bernardino National Forest.

Standing in front of the cabin steps were four people who radiated kindness. The older woman held a microphone and led everyone to a community area behind the cabin. More gigantic pines surrounded a beautiful set of picnic tables and chairs overlooking the brilliance of the forest. A huge area in the middle centered on a firepit, and everyone was instructed to head toward the stage.

"Okay, everyone, my name is Karry, and this is my husband, Robert. We are the camp directors here. These two are our children: Chrissy, who is a counselor here, and little Jane. We are all going to find seats around the benches to eat lunch and find out who your counselor is!"

Sandwiches, milk, and snacks were passed around as Pretzel took over to call out kids' names and the counselors they were assigned. I couldn't believe it, but JerBear was my counselor! All the kids he had ran over to sit with him behind the firepit, and I sat right next to him.

"What's up, champ!" he said loudly.

I just smiled.

We then were assigned cabins with metal bunk beds, and we were asked to change into swim trunks so the day could begin with a fun time at the pool. I was embarrassed since I was so small but got over it, as all the kids were in the pool or around it together. Even the counselors got in.

A whistle ended pool time, and the counselors wanted kids to take showers in turns by cabin number. The shower stalls were in their cabin area, and the water was bitterly cold. It warmed up eventually, but not much, and I couldn't wait to get out of there for dinner.

Dinner was served at the tables outside, and the ants were big, black, and menacing. They were everywhere.

JerBear warned us to watch our feet and not drop food, but that was impossible. The directors had a happy mutt running around everywhere that was supersweet, but we were instructed not to feed him. Who could say no to puppy eyes?

We spent days singing, eating, swimming, hiking, and being kind to one another. On the third night, JerBear's group of kids were given the option to come up to the campfire and accept God. I had seen the beautiful exchange the night before, and I wanted to do it so badly, but fear got the better of me.

My counselor knew and sat close to me that night. He was kind and encouraging, and I felt like everyone was staring at me. Jane, the daughter of the directors, hung out with me and made me rings out of colorful string. She was more mature than me and whispered in my ear, "Jeremy, you don't have to do it if you don't want to, but God wants you to."

On JerBear's nudge, I slowly stood up when they asked us if anyone wanted to accept the Lord as their savior. I had my head down and couldn't describe my trepidation. I walked up, holding JerBear's hand, and the director took my other hand as he said, "Jeremy, we are so proud of you for being brave and accepting."

The fire raged warmly behind me, and the smoke made it hard to see everyone gathered around, but I felt them. The director, holding his well-worn, brown-cased Bible, soothed my anxiety by sitting down with me around the fire and explaining to me what it means to be a servant of God.

At nine years old, I didn't know much, but I accepted him into my little heart that summer night in 1990. What made everything real was his presence. That feeling made me burst into tears, and then everyone around me cheered.

Jane was there next to me, and I could see little tears in her big brown eyes. Jerbear was right there, too, as were many others. It felt right, and I knew I did the right thing. God was in my heart and soul, where he would always be.

Beautiful days blended with morning praise and singing in the amphitheater after breakfast. Even in the summer, those mornings were brisk, and there were birds flying everywhere. On the first day, we had received Bible study packets and assignments to do every day.

We worked on these with our counselors and had private time to go over our answers. We took stunning hikes into the woods, and honest conversations about what the scripture meant filled our hearts.

On the last night, we worked in groups to perform a skit in front of everyone at the fire and had the entire week to practice. I remember vividly what our group acted out: the killer glove.

The premise was, a baseball glove kids found on the floor had a mind of its own. The kid would think they found a cool new glove and put it on; then it would come alive in their hand. It would attack them—their face and everything around them—until they could get it off.

Nobody wanted to say goodbye, and everyone wanted to stay friends. Getting close over God and campfires was eternal, but it was also fleeting. We had final praise to the Lord in the amphitheater and then grouped up by the buses near the front of the cabin after grabbing our belongings from the cozy huts we called home.

Tears flowed down my face saying goodbye to the directors and their daughters, but mostly JerBear. He held my hand all the way to the bus, but most of the counselors had to stay for after-camp leadership instruction.

That amazing week at Camp Annandale would not be the last time I visited and experienced such beautiful humanity.

CHAPTER 16

ROBBER

Costa Mesa, California, 1990–1991

The mentality and behavior of drug addicts and alcoholics is wholly irrational until you understand that they are completely powerless over their addiction.
—RUSSELL BRAND

On a beautiful day at the park near Traverse, in midsummer, my world changed forever.

During the weekdays, Mama Reata oversaw the art we did on the park benches, and while most of the kids played sports, I spent my time luxuriously drawing something with Mama Reata.

These were times I cherished with Mama Reata and the art she taught. She was so talented and had a passion for bringing out my creative gene. There was never a moment she got annoyed with my questions or when I messed up a drawing. Her patience led me toward a path that forever centered around creativity.

Even when she was not around, I would draw or color or do something artistic to make her proud of me. But on this day at that park, even her amazing soul could not stop what was about to happen.

•••

Time slowed as the Saint's minivan drove into the park.

His car moved as slow as clouds in a windless sky, and when he parked, he didn't get out. Mama Reata and I faced the parking area, with the huge field behind us, while we all waited for Bob to get out of the van.

Then the Cajun's green truck drove up just as slowly and deliberately. He usually didn't come to these functions. It was an indication something was wrong, and at this time nothing pointed toward me.

Why would it? My mother was out of the picture, getting better in a halfway house. My father's side of the family didn't care where I was. My grandpa was nothing but perfect to me.

Then my grandfather's ranger drove up a few minutes later. He jumped out and immediately locked eyes with me. There was danger and pain in his eyes—something I had never seen in him.

Mama Reata put her arm around me instinctively and held on tight. I was smashed into her side, and I knew something terrible had happened. I knew it was my mom, but I just didn't know what or why.

I felt my heart in every part of my body, and I couldn't breathe. I didn't want to look up, and I didn't want Mama Reata to let me go. She held me as I began to shake.

Everything was going to fall apart again. They were going to take me back to Orangewood. I must have done something wrong again, or the treatment for my tummy was not enough. Or I had stayed too long, and they needed the space for another neglected kid.

Nothing made sense, and time just laughed at me in his slow-moving silence.

Mama Reata stirred and felt the hot tears peel off her shirt as she tried to move me away. I could not look up, and I closed my eyes. I would not let them take me away again. I would run away.

I felt a hand on my shoulder and knew it was my grandpa's. His engineer hands were huge and calloused. There was nothing but affection there, and I felt time's slithering grasp on me weaken.

I transferred my devastating hug onto my grandpa's leg and would not open my eyes. "Please don't take me back to Orangewood, please," I begged over and over as he patted my curly head.

"Jeremy, it's okay, big boy. You are not going back to Orangewood. I would never let that happen again, okay?" my grandfather said slowly, the whole time patting my hair.

Mama Reata was rubbing my back gently in circles.

If I was not going back to Orangewood, why were they here? Everyone I loved was around me; Bob and Bill were on the other side of the park bench. There was a silence that shook my entire body.

Maybe I could just hide in my grandpa's embrace forever and never know the bad things that were ahead of me. I knew it was not to be. I knew my grandpa, Reata, Bill, and Bob Ford needed me to be brave. So I looked up with tears streaming down my face.

●●●

Crystalized tears tugged at my eyes, but I fought through the fear and extinguished the immobilization in my heart. The Cajun and the Saint looked miserable; they had sadness and despair written all over their bodies.

Standing close to Grandpa, I squeezed his hand. Mama Reata held my other hand in a motherly embrace. The Cajun was fidgeting from one foot to the other, and I could see tears in his eyes as he looked down on me across that forlorn park bench. The Saint was trying to remain composed in his dress clothes but was struggling.

Silence blossomed, and the carnal pain radiated around us without an ability to dissipate. The once thick clouds in the sky seemed to droop, and the breeze was gone. What was happening if I was not going back to Orangewood?

"Hey, buddy, I know you are confused, but we need you to be brave," the Saint said slowly.

I looked up at my grandpa, and he smiled sadly. This was bad.

"It's about your mother, Jeremy. She was caught robbing a bank," the Saint said in a low voice while leaning over the park table.

I didn't know what to say. How could she do this?

"We are here for you, no matter what—me, your grandpa, Reata, and Bill. We will never let you be alone, okay?" the Saint said, his eyes misty.

I sat down and put my head between my arms so they couldn't see me cry.

Mama Reata pulled me close again, and my grandpa sat down next to me, whispering everything was okay, and I was safe with them.

I didn't feel fine. I didn't feel anything. Just cold.

Cold crept up through my legs in staggering chills and ended with icicles in my heart. There was nothing for me to say and no reason to cry anymore.

My mother had robbed a bank. She was the getaway driver and got caught. She also had heroin on her. She was put in a women's jail near Orangewood, awaiting arraignment to move to prison.

I was never going to see her again, and I was going to live the rest of my young life in group homes.

I stood up and hugged each one of them. I needed to be alone and walked away toward the basketball court. Then I ran. I ran without looking back or listening to them yelling for me.

I ran to the basketball court and didn't stop there. I kept going. Tears I was trying to hold back came forward like twin waterfalls.

Once I got past the courts, I kept walking, running toward the main street, Paularino. We were not supposed to go there, and it was considered running away if we did. I didn't care.

There was an Asian market up the road called Yohan, and they had cool Japanese arcade games. I was going there and kept walking with tears uncontrollably flowing down my red face.

They let me go and knew I wouldn't run away. I knew I wouldn't run away, and Yohan was a lot farther than I thought.

Crossing the street to get to the supermarket, I realized I didn't have any change and just stood there looking at the parking lot. Then I saw my grandpa's truck, and he was stoic in his pain for me. I walked over and appreciated that he had waited in the truck for me.

We just sat there, not talking, and I cuddled up to him to just cry. He let me and held me without saying anything. Poor Grandpa didn't sign up for that, and I couldn't imagine the pain he felt for me. He didn't deserve that either.

The familiar smells of his aftershave and the oil from the truck brought me back to reality. We didn't drive back to the park but went straight back to the group home, where everyone was waiting for me in awkward sadness. The Saint, the Cajun, Mama Reata, and the Flash were waiting outside, worried for me.

My grandpa asked me to grab some clothes to stay the night with him. I had never got to sleepover at his house, and that shocked me back into my resilient self.

"Go ahead and get extra clothes. Bob approved you staying over Friday night as well as Saturday. He feels this is the best time to start. How does that sound?" he asked with a wry grin and sad eyes.

For a moment, I forgot how my mother had abandoned me, permanently, and I smiled through bloodshot eyes and said, "Really? Yes!"

God blessed me with resilience, and no matter the situation, I bounced back. Walking over to those who truly cared about me gave me solace, and they all embraced me with love. They cared deeply for me, and I felt so lucky to have that.

Mama Reata and the Cajun took me to collect my backpack for the long weekend with my grandpa. "Where are the other kids?" I asked inquisitively.

"They are in the living room with Sandy. He wanted to say bye to you before you leave with your grandpa, okay?" Reata said with a slow smile on her pretty face.

"Okay," I said.

Smokey gave me a big bear hug, and I remember him tearing up as he told me, "No matter what, Jeremy, we are here for you."

Starting to cry again, I held on to him as he walked me out the door to my grandpa, who was waiting patiently for me in his Ranger.

There was no one I would have rather been with than my grandpa and Bella. They never once let me down, and when I was with them, it was easy to pretend I was not a group home kid in an unforgiving world.

Jeremy,

Hi sweetheart! I hope your
feeling better. I just want you to
know that I love you more then
anything in this world.

Being able to talk with you
makes things alot better. I miss you
very much honey. I don't know exactly
how long its going to take, but we
will be together again.

I'm so proud of you. your aunt
Sherry sent me some pictures & I
look at them everyday. you are a
very handsome young man but I
bet you already know that. Did
you have a nice time in San Diego?
when I spoke to you on the phone I
didn't understand why you didn't
go to Sea World. Did you go to the zoo?

Time goes by pretty slow here, but
Its given me time to get my thinking
straight. you are the most important
part of my life and I thank God that
he has given me the chance to make
things right with you. Now all I want
is to be with you & be the best mom
I can be. I love you so much, with all
my heart & soul. Belive me Jeremy, not
Drugs or anything will separate us
again.
                    always, mom.

CHAPTER 17

GRANDPA

Huntington Beach, California, 1991

━━━━━━━━━━━━━━

*Being deeply loved by someone gives you strength, while loving
someone deeply gives you courage.*
—LAO TZU

Every which way the truck turned, I felt the heat of the sun on my
face. Driving away from the Traverse home with my grandpa, I
felt drained, exposed, and sad. My eyes held tears that were ready
to fall again every few minutes. Overwhelmed with emotion, I
leaned my head against the door and fell asleep listening to the
engine rumble softly.

Feeling the truck stop gently, I opened my eyes, and we were
at Grandpa's house. The sun was lower in the sky, and my stomach
growled at me in rage. Grandpa nudged me to open the door with
a smile and said, "Let's go see what Bella made for dinner!"

Walking up to his perfect home and seeing the light green
lagoon in the background, their beautiful foliage, and colorful
plants helped me forget my mother had robbed a bank. She was

no longer a part of my life.

The decadent aroma of pasta sauce hit us as he opened the door, and we both smiled. We loved her pasta, and Bella knew how much I could eat. I am sure she knew what was going on, and I could hear her in the kitchen cooking.

Her passions were Italian food and cooking. She got so much enjoyment out of seeing her family and friends eating the delicious foods. It radiated from her as she overfilled plates. There was not a thing she cooked I didn't like.

When I walked around the corner to see Bella, she immediately flew over to me and hugged me into her so hard I couldn't breathe. I felt her crying, and it made me cry. She knew about my mom, for sure.

"Oh, Jeremy, we are here and love you. I am so sorry to hear about your mama," Bella said, out of breath from crying. She smelled like her flowery perfume, olive oil, and tomatoes.

"Guess what I am making for you?" she asked sweetly.

"Pasta and red sauce?" I asked, remembering how to say it. It was not Italian food or spaghetti or noodles. It was pasta and red sauce, and she would not let me forget.

Bella hummed to herself as she smiled at me and messed up my hair before walking back to the sauce. She had to constantly monitor and stir it, or it would burn. Everything she did in the kitchen she told me, and I loved helping her cook.

Grandpa brought over a small stool and put it in front of the sauce so I could stir. He smiled and walked over to the table in the breakfast nook, attached to the kitchen, to smoke a cigarette with a novel. He loved to read, and I never saw him with the same book.

"Remember: stir from the outside in and then inside out in a circular pattern. Don't let it stick to the sides, baby," she told me every time, no matter what. The sauce is what makes the pasta, even when it is a perfect al dente.

I gleefully stirred and stirred.

While I helped in the kitchen, my grandpa sat watching and lovingly talking to Bella. He called her Dutch, and I never knew why, other than it was a sweet thing he said when calling for her. My grandpa was kind to me and never once raised his voice other than to call out to see where we were.

He had a beautiful grandfather clock that he wound up on Sunday mornings. It sat in the corner of the huge two-story living room, and the polished wood reflected the sparkling lagoon behind it. Looking at that clock reminded me of the time I was given with him and how lucky I truly was.

His ability to provide love and complete attention to a child who was not related to him was beyond selfless. He had a big family, with lots of grandkids who would visit, but mostly it was the two of us hanging out together on weekends. When the other kids came over, he made sure to keep me around so I didn't feel out of place.

Grandpa had four children—three boys and one daughter.

Frank was the oldest son. He served in Vietnam and later became a career K9 detective. Frank had an uncanny fear of spiders, big or small, all thanks to the dank rainforests of Vietnam. He had a love for the ocean and owned a sailboat with his wife, Marina. In retirement, they would sail to the Caribbean. Grandpa was very proud of him and their two kids—Frank Jr. (Franky) and

Marlana—who were always kind to me.

Franky and his wife, Noelle, were the cool ones. They were the life of the party at Grandpa's and fun to be around. Franky and Marlana loved their dad, and it showed in how they doted on him. Big Frank let me bother him like I did Grandpa and was always patient.

Maria was the second oldest, the only girl, and was very much like her mother, Bella. Maria and her husband, Tim, had four daughters. There was not a single moment when I felt like I didn't belong. Maria was a nurse, and Tim worked in an audio-technical field.

Tim was always mechanical and a kind man who loved to smile. Their four daughters never made me feel alone or unwanted.

Christina was the oldest of Tim and Maria's children; she was a rebel I had a secret crush on. Then Lauren was my age, mature and tall. Third came Jessica, who I had the most in common with. She never pitied me and was genuinely curious as to where I came from. Lindsey was the youngest and a sweet girl.

My grandfather spoiled his grandchildren, and they loved him fiercely. He enjoyed seeing my interaction with them and how close we all became. I was not a biological grandkid, but they all took me in when I had nothing.

"Jeremy, Jessica, and Lauren are looking for you outside," he would holler at me every time they came to visit. Those two girls were kind to me and let me play with them outside on the public swings. Christina enjoyed helping her mom and Bella in the kitchen making pasta but made time for me.

Bill, Grandpa's third child, was in real estate, loved guns, and had a horse ranch. He was a confident man who went through a tough divorce. He had three boys, all of whom had very unique personalities and enjoyed being around the family. I loved being around this close-knit family.

Brett was Bill's oldest, who later joined the air force, and he loved to roughhouse with me. Then there was William, who ended up becoming an aviator in the air force. Eric was the youngest and loved skateboarding. I was not as close to them but wanted to be.

Robert, the youngest, was married to a French woman, Nadine. She was mean to everyone. Robert was a psychologist for the Green Bay Packers and lived in Wisconsin. He had a son named Alex, who was quiet and stayed near his mother most of the time. When they came to visit, we all tried to be there.

Robert passed away from cancer a few years later, and it was heartbreaking to everyone. He loved his family and was especially close to Bella. Robert always found time for me and enjoyed seeing his dad become a CASA. I remember visiting them in Green Bay and how inviting they were.

When all the family were together, or just a few, we would play cards. The main games were hearts and gin rummy. Bella would play those games with just me before the family arrived so I knew the rules.

There were gallons of wine flowing around, and Bella always said, "Put it in the fridge, Jeremy. When it's cold, it tastes better!"

The laughter and time together would make its way out into the backyard patio, where the grandkids took turns on the paddleboat. On days the family came over, Bella asked me to help her weed the garden, which I did happily. As the sun settled, Grandpa would bring out raw hot dogs on a string to tease out the sand sharks in the glistening lagoon.

That lagoon brought peace, and I could see all the other homes across the water. It was a gentle reprieve before driving back to the home.

Once the pink sun completely set, everyone went inside, with the adults at the large dinner table in the dining room overlooking the living room. The kids would sit at the table in the breakfast nook or the den, if space was filled up. I liked to sit in the den because sometimes I felt like I was intruding.

They never led me to feel that way; I just felt I didn't belong in such a beautiful family setting as a group home kid. That transition back to reality came Sunday evening, when Grandpa would have to drop me back off at the Traverse home.

It never got better.

The cold grasp of group home life and reality was painful. Bob hated it, too, and would draw out the happy evenings, if possible.

Bella would rarely drive with us unless we were going from the group home to Maria and Tim's house in Lake Forest. If that were the case, she would be there in their big blue Cadillac Fleetwood, lounging in the back seat with a comfy blanket. I loved that blue boat and how comfy the white leather seats were.

Going to Maria's was always a great Saturday. She had two golden retrievers who were loving and playful. I believe one was called Nala, but I can't be sure. Grandpa had their wiener dog, Feedy, but he was a one-owner animal, and he loved his dad. Feedy would put up with me and sometimes lay with me in the den, but only if my grandpa was close.

Tim and his daughters liked to watch movies or hang out in their backyard, enjoying the midday California sun. We never spent the night and would leave after dinner to get back to Huntington Beach, which was around thirty minutes each way. Grandpa would drink a cup of black coffee and drive, with Bella in the back seat reading a magazine or *Reader's Digest.*

Bella would make me café au lait in the mornings, and I loved that special time with her. It was a mocha that used boiled milk and instant coffee in a pot, but with her touch it was magic. It was delicious and made me feel special. Grandpa would make fun of me and tease me as I drank it.

"Men drink their coffee black, Jeremy," he would say while tickling me.

Bella would walk over and refill his coffee with a smirk and roll her eyes at me. I believe my presence there on the weekends was as much a comfort to them as it was to me. Their children and grandchildren were not around as much. Maybe that was based on family dynamics, but all the same, it was sad. I hated thinking of them alone during the weekdays and wished I could live with them permanently.

Having the weekends to look forward to with the Butlers changed the way I saw life in the group homes. My grandparents gave me unconditional love and affection when I needed it most. Their selfless acts saved a group home kid from feeling alone and unloved.

There would never be a moment when I was not grateful for what they gave me. They saved me and gave me a home. A life filled with love.

It made the drab group home weekdays much easier to get through.

Jeremy Bracamontes
Stephanie Caldera
Aaron Campbell
Abel Cortes
Nicholas Crane

Loan Do
Thang Do
Thao Duong
Kenneth Green
Garrett Hefley

Samantha Judkins
Melissa Kearney
Mina Ly
Bradley McEvoy
Alejandra Mendiola

Hanh Nguyen
Paul Nguyen
Katie Park
Dung Pham
Sandra Sandoval

Christine Sauceda
Gemma Thompson-Hail
Thanh Tran
Kittrell Travis
Phuc Vu

John Wallace
Christopher W

SONORA'S PLAYERS

Mrs. Bonnie Fevergeon, former Sonora teacher, coordinates our Drama Club every Wednesday after school.

Drama

SONORA SCHOOL
1991-1992

CHAPTER 18

ALONE

Costa Mesa, 1991–1992

––––––––––––

Loneliness is my least favorite thing about life. The thing that I'm most worried about is just being alone without anybody to care for or someone who will care for me.

—ANNE HATHAWAY

Delicate letters written from a dark prison in Long Beach were my only connection to a mom who lost her freedom due to stupid decisions. Those personal notes had intricate drawings of Mickey Mouse and other Disney characters, showing off her wasted creative talents—grim reminders of a time lost with my mother.

Empty promises and hollow assurances about making things right disintegrated what was left of my optimistic outlook on life outside the home. I had two pictures of her, and both were from within the prison. I could see the massive concrete walls and barbed wire in the background.

She was not in prison garb and stood next to a big tree, limiting the feel of jail life. It did the opposite. I had them tacked near the front of my bed and no longer looked at them every night. My mom was slowly becoming a memory that had no substance.

She was lost to the venomous world of felons and incarceration. Her return flight to the land of sobriety and freedom left without her swiftly. I was smart enough to know that living with her would have been devastating, and it was no longer a pipe dream I held close.

Her sentence was ten years, and by that time I would be well on my way to figuring out my own life. Knowing this, she was still unwilling to give up her parental rights.

Due to this, I could not be put up for adoption.

Most families wanted newborns or toddlers to adopt, but that doesn't take away from those left behind. Many of the kids in the homes would eventually go back to their families or extended relatives, but a few, including myself, had no prospects for a normal life.

At the Traverse home, all the original crew had left, besides Peter. My long tenure and good behavior had secured more trust but without true freedom. Peter, as he got older, became harder to deal with due to his increased seizures and had to have his brain shunt drained more often.

I worried about him constantly, and he would say my name during some of his episodes. It was tormenting to watch when they held him down, put a stick in his mouth to protect his tongue, and tried to weather the storm.

Grandpa stayed with me throughout all trauma and emotional breakdowns, but he was not able to dedicate the time it takes to parent a soon-to-be teenage boy. Seventh grade at Costa Mesa

High School—"Mesa"—prompted the deepest and darkest fears I could think of.

●●●

The change happened all at once. A metamorphosis of loss.

The Cajun, my great friend, was leaving, and it felt like something inside me was about to break. Mama Reata had been offered a wonderful job back in New York, where she was from, and was leaving.

She gave me her drafting table. I knew how much it meant to her, and I cherished it dearly. The table had a white top covered in ink and paint marks. It opened up on squeaky gold hinges. I loved to hide my most prized possessions inside, like my calculator watch. She had left me drawing pens with nice paper inside that I used every day. It was a way for her to say goodbye, knowing a piece of her would stay with me, and it did.

Having been so close to her, sharing her love for art and seeing how this opportunity made her smile, allowed me to let her go. My selfishness only led up to the deep sadness in my heart from losing her, but she could not be an hourly paid staff member forever. I knew this.

I would miss her more than anyone I had ever met.

On the days after school, my Reata used to be there. I would find reasons to stay in my room and draw. Losing the last truly close woman in my life, besides Bella, put another crack in my little heart. She wrote to me many times, and I could tell it broke her heart to say goodbye.

Rebecca and Keith Nogy replaced Bill Turner as houseparents

right before I started seventh grade. I was not sure where the Cajun was going, but the Saint promoted from within, and his second-in-charge, Kathy, needed help.

"I will still be around, Jeremy, and you can always call me," he said while handing me a gift. It was a set of Staedtler Mars drawing templates that I had been wanting. I remember him hugging me and having to walk away due to the tears.

The Nogys were kind, but distant.

They came with so much personal property; it filled the entire two-car garage to the point we could barely do laundry in there. They also had a cat they kept in the upstairs loft that was their living space. I could smell the cat or its litter box close by in the dining-room kitchen.

They were a different kind of houseparent, to say the least. Keith was rarely involved and had another job that kept him away all day. Rebecca liked to do crafts but had a low patience threshold. She was caring and would sometimes read stories in the hallway to us boys before bed.

When they took over and realized how long I had been there, they tasked me with too much responsibility.

"Hey, Jeremy, we need you to help us make sure the kids are staying at school and tell us if they are ditching," Rebecca once asked. She also wanted me to keep tabs on the kids if they stayed up without permission at night.

"No way," I had said, and it strained my relationship with them. It was also a time I realized I had a strong moral compass.

The Nogys were trying to do the right thing by following rules. This included telling them what was going on with the other kids when they were not around, and I could not do it. It felt wrong, and growing up the way we did, ratting on someone was one of the lowest things we could do.

I told Rebecca one day, "I don't want to be the responsible kid in the house who you ask for help or to tell on others!"

After that, she left me alone, and we never acted the same toward each other.

I was lonely for a long time after Mama Reata and the Cajun left. Flash was let go for who knows what, and Patty left when she got married. Michelle moved to another city that was too far of a commute. The psychologists had been less inclined to personalize their relationships with the kids, but it stung to see them move on.

Smokey came by occasionally, but his focus was the Paularino home, as most of those kids were his responsibility. Dr. Newman also made her quarterly visits, but for the most part, it was an isolated existence. My grandpa and Bella could not take me every weekend due to family obligations stemming from medical issues, which was hard for me to understand.

Although I was a part of their family, I was never really their family. Grandpa did his best to hide that fact from me, but it was very obvious when the grandchildren were there. They deserved attention too.

I found myself falling into something not bright enough to smile through. I wasn't sad for long and had a carefree attitude, but middle school was shaking me to the core.

I was resilient, and it made me who I was. Other kids had trouble getting over things and held on to negative energy. Even the most painful things never kept me down and only made me stronger.

Most nights, listening to the night staff members' TV show whispering in the living room, I would wonder if my mom was thinking of me at the same time. It kept me from hating her. I remember those horrible nights she got so high in Bernie's bathroom and would pass out for hours.

Heroin took her soul to Hades, and prison was her hell on earth. The other kids I knew in the homes had parents who were addicts, but for the most part, they cleaned up their acts for the sake of their children. That is why so many kids passed through in just a few months.

I was going on five years at the Traverse home and had seen dozens of kids fill the five other beds. One kid named Shawn Lewis was there going on a year, and it was the longest tenure, besides when Peter was there. Shawn was a charismatic kid about a year younger than me but way bigger.

We went on a group home camping trip to Catalina Island over one weekend. I was so excited to get on the ferry and start an adventure. The Saint and Kathy were there too. There were multiple group homes in the camping park, including an all-girls home, which I had never heard of before. This was when I found out who Shawn was.

Earlier that day, we all hiked up Blackjack Mountain to see the wild buffalo on the plateau overlooking the Pacific Ocean and the beautiful, dark blue crushing coast of California. It was an amazing experience.

We could see into tomorrow, and the sun glistened off the face of the ocean, making me squint. It reminded me of all the stars in the sky, and I could not believe how beautiful it was.

Once we got to the top, we ate buffalo burgers and lounged around. Shawn began acting differently toward me. At first I thought he was just tired, but I watched him and realized he was very interested in one of the girls from the other home.

Things changed that evening at the base of the mountain.

That moonless night, around a fire, everything was silent but the persistent buzz of insects. We could hear the wild boar in the dry bush not far off and some whispering from the kids. Besides Shawn, I shadowed the Saint, who was sitting quietly next to Kathy.

Since there was nowhere to run off to, our only rule was to not go anywhere alone. Shawn knew this and made sure Bob saw him ask me to go with him to another fire. I knew which fire he wanted to go to, and it made me uncomfortable, but I went anyway.

I stood stupidly near a eucalyptus tree while he talked and flirted with one of the Latina girls in the other home. He looked at me many times, winking and making stupid signs with his hands, but I just wanted to go back to our fire.

So stupidly I said, "Hey, Shawn, can we go back? It's cold out here."

Rage filled his eyes, and darkness spread over his face. His crazy smile terrified me. I backed up. I was too far from the Saint, and he knew it.

"I am gonna fuck you up, pussy!" he whispered and lunged toward me.

Regretfully, I turned my back on him to run away, and that was a painful misjudgment. He pushed me so hard I went flying and hit the dirt and lost my breath. Before I could scream, he pushed my face in the dirt and rocks while holding me down with a knee to my spine.

Shawn held me there for what seemed like forever, then leaned down and said, "Fuck you, and you better not rat."

He let me up, and then when I turned toward him, he pushed me one more time for good measure. This time my knee landed on a cactus, and I cried out. He just laughed and walked over to the girl, who was also laughing.

I held in my tears as I felt the barbs push through my jeans. He got her group home phone number and slithered back toward me to make sure we walked back to the fire together. We didn't say a word to each other, but I felt betrayed.

My lip swelled, and blood was metallic on my tongue as I tried to test the pain. Making sure to sit in the shadows, I never looked up so the Saint couldn't see me. Shawn glared at me with a grin most of the night, and I thanked God he was not in my tent.

Once I got to my tent and had a flashlight, I looked at my injured leg. The other kid in the tent just looked at me and rolled over. He knew the rules of the jungle.

I grabbed pliers from the toolbox on the picnic bench and did my best to pull out the cactus needles without screaming. There were only a dozen or so that were big; the invisible smaller ones were going to have to fall out on their own, and it was going to be a painful night.

I had a few baby wipes I used to clean my face and looked through the tent window to see the Saint and Kathy, still by the fire, smiling about something. Besides getting beat up, Catalina was a fun trip, and it was great getting some attention from the owner of the group home.

That next morning we were all set to get back on the ferry toward Newport Beach, and the Saint asked, "Want to sit next to me and Kathy on the boat, buddy?"

Smiling, I said, "Yes, please!"

I saw Shawn in the background, flipping me off with one hand and putting a finger to his throat with the other.

I never told on Shawn, and we didn't hang out anymore after that at the home. He had a CASA, too, who was in her forties and was going to adopt him. As much as I hated how he treated me, I was happy he got a chance to have a family.

Back to the isolation and back to the world of lost kids. That was better than getting my ass beat and cactus stuck in my leg.

This is just a couple of picture of me, I gave you two. When I gave you these pictures I was at my Casa's house sorting other picture, I have to go know so I hope you like this quick note and picture. Love you!

Sincerly,
your only son,
Jeremy

XOXOX
XOXOX

P.S please write back. OH ya! my casa said, "hello," and so did his wife, there real nice.

CHAPTER 19

SHACKLES

Long Beach, 1992

Orphans are easier to ignore before you know their names;
but once you do, everything changes.
—DAVID PLATT

Hiding within the cold embrace of the courtroom's toneless pews, I saw my estranged mother for the first time since visiting her in prison when I was ten. The social worker next to me was a sentinel in a suit, protecting me from the pain I had already felt. My mom's vivid orange jumpsuit popped with color comparatively to the stark onyx bars of her prison box.

"All rise," the bailiff announced as the black-robed judge took his seat with direct purpose.

Shackled from her jail-issued white shoes to her once beautiful hands, the feeling of isolation was profound. I had not touched her since I was six and felt the full weight of her presence in the broken pieces of my twelve-year-old heart. Her ravaged face hid behind a wild mane of brown hair that had once been the envy of every woman. She knew I was there.

"Please be seated," the stoic judge responded.

The sound of everyone taking their seat reminded me how full the courtroom was, and the silence that ensued tugged at my trampled soul.

My mother glanced back every few minutes, deliberately and toward where I huddled, directly behind the lawyer's table. That directed movement caused her iron chains to clang piercingly against the dark cage that held her eternal shame. I could not look at her long and felt tears cascade down my cheeks.

"Do I have to be here?" I asked the social worker. He was not Mike but still very caring.

He put his arm around me and said, "It will be over soon, Jeremy. You are so brave."

She would not see me when she was in prison again; her embarrassment trumped love. She did not want to look at me from behind a piece of glass but would call the group home pretending things were going to be okay. Before that trial, my social worker had to lie and tell her the district attorney needed her statement for parental rights.

It was a mistake to visit her.

My mother looked beaten and worn down when we pretended to be legal counsel a few years back. Her dark hair was wet from a shower, and there was no emotion on her tired face. When she saw me from behind the glass instead of a suit, she froze in anguish. She froze in fear and shame.

Her tears and shaking made a connection with me impossible. My mother could not handle looking at me, so she abandoned the conversation. The screeching of the red plastic chair as she pushed it back silenced everyone around, and the alert guard with the baton in the back immediately focused in on her. Her shaking hands came up to request handcuffs, and she didn't look back.

We never spoke. She didn't pick up the phone. She left me as before.

The phone connecting our worlds sat limply on the other side of the glass, while I still held mine. All those loving letters and hollow promises echoed in my mind. I hung up the plastic phone slowly, with my head down, and cried on the shoulder of that poor social worker.

"Mommy!" I had yelled over and over, but to no avail.

She never turned back and walked out the door on quickened steps. Her hair flowed down her back and left wet imprints on her dark gray jumpsuit.

Soggy air saluted me as we walked out of the visitor control area of the prison in Long Beach. We maneuvered past the multiple guard posts that welcomed visitors through beeping metal detectors. People formed in a line, waiting to enter to see loved ones, but I would never come back. She had turned her back on me.

"Let's get you out of here, bud," the social worker said, and I had no response but to lower my head in grief. He guided me toward the exit and what was my left of my mother.

Vivid recall from that life-destroying day brought me back to the old courtroom, and I didn't want to look at her anymore. I pushed myself behind the social worker so my mom could not see me and wished my grandpa was there to take me away.

The court benches were worn to a shiny hue and had seen their share of visitors over the years. My short legs dangled over, without touching the ground.

My mother lost her parental rights that day. She was unfit to be a mother. She was a convicted felon, failed bank robber, and a heroin addict. She had chased down the little sanity she had left from inside a bottle of whatever alcohol was available.

I never saw her again.

In the lobby, outside where my mother was caged and past the security area, the Saint was waiting to take me back to the Traverse house.

"Jeremy, my boy, want to get some In-N-Out burgers?" the Saint said jovially.

He always tried to lighten the situation, and I couldn't resist a hug from him. "Yes, please," I spoke.

I wanted to hold his hand but felt like I was getting too old. I loved the mustard-grilled patties and the milkshakes at In-N-Out. The drive from Long Beach to Costa Mesa was not that bad, but the whole ride my heart continued to break.

After that courtroom visit, I was put up for adoption. I was too old and going on thirteen so didn't put much thought into it. My days went back to normal, and my weekends were full of love at the Butlers', but I still could not cut out the thought of my shadow of a mother.

She had lost everything to heroin and had admitted to my social worker that robbing a bank was her ticket to a life with her son. Even I saw through the ridiculousness of that comment, but I never forgot it. In her confused eyes, that was the only way she could justify the deed that cost her son.

One weekend, after a delicious meal at Arby's, where my grandpa tried unsuccessfully to include Horsey Sauce on my sandwich, I got a surprise call.

Bella had found my grandmother on my mom's side phone number through the CASA network and wanted my grandmother to know she had a sweet grandson. The conversation with her didn't go well.

"Jeremy, your grandmother is on the phone and would like to speak to you," Bella said, with her hand covering the phone.

"What do I say?" I whispered back.

Bella just smiled and offered me the phone. My grandpa sat at the kitchen table, focused on me but holding a book. I do not remember the conversation. I do remember my grandmother's voice; it was cold and cruel.

After the call, Bella sat me down with my grandpa. She looked sad and resigned. Something was wrong.

"Jeremy, I am so sorry, but you won't be speaking to your grandmother anymore. She told me her heart was still broken from your mom and her sister, Sherri. She told me to tell you she would always think of you but could not take care of you," Bella said softly.

Both my mother and her sister broke their family apart. Their drug-and-alcohol addictions caused turmoil. I found out my mother's father committed suicide before I was born, but I'm not sure why or how.

I shrugged and said, "Well, you are my grandmother anyway."

Bella started crying and pulled me in close. We never spoke

about my mother's mom again, and it helped heal a wound that would not close.

That summer was hard, but Costa Mesa High School was going to be another hard-fought battle of survival.

February 10, 1992

Dear Mom,
"Hi! How are you doing, I'm doing fine. For some reason I always start my letters this way but that's not the subject. Your getting out in 18 days, can you believe it, I can't! I love you so much I can't wait to see you. I know the halfway house is going to be really hard but I know you can change in there. I had a basketball game Friday and we won by 6 points, we haven't lost a game yet. If you do well... I can... you in... to a... you... write... house... live with... 6 months... year. I love... very much.

P.S. write back
love you
XOXOX
OXOXO

Sincerely,
your only son
Jeremy

CHAPTER 20

MESA

Costa Mesa, 1992–1993

━━━━━━━━━━━

The worst cruelty that can be inflicted on a human
being is isolation.
—SUKARNO

I walked unsteadily toward a new bus stop. Without a staff member
to guide me, I was haunted by the Juniors of a time past beating
me up. Wearing one of Smokey's light blue flannel shirts, which
surprisingly didn't look like a dress on me, I walked alone. The bus
for middle school and high school at Mesa stopped at the end of
the main connecting road, Paularino.

It felt like a mile away, and it was where I ran after finding out
my mom had robbed a bank. Yohan was right up the road.

Cool air brushed through my eyelashes, and I looked up to see
fast-moving clouds in a sky that had barely been touched by the
rising sun. Beady-eyed crows lined the many electric wires like
gangsters holding down territories from wanton rivals. I feared
their well-aimed bomber arsenal.

I could see a horde of kids waiting ahead of me. My old sneakers slowed, my pulse quickened, realizing there was no going back, and I had to do this.

I was the oldest in the Traverse home, and the other kids were still in grade school. The newly forged freedom the Saint awarded me was based on trust and not causing problems. I did not want to abuse that or not do the right thing.

The first day at Mesa made my stomach turn into a knot of despair.

I got close to the bus stop and saw at least a dozen kids laughing together. I knew there was no place for me. These kids grew up together and had formed bonds. Group home kids were not allowed this type of interaction and could not invite friends over.

We did not have friends.

Standing back in the darkness, between spicy-smelling pine trees, I blended with the obscurity waiting for the bus. Nobody noticed me, and it was easy to hide when nobody was looking for me.

Fearing a bully amid the bus stop, I made sure to remain silent. It felt like hours passed before the huge yellow Blue Bird bus squealed its way to a stop, and the kids yelled joyfully, pushing on to the bus. I was the last one on and became visible.

There were no seats. There were seats, but nobody shared.

A boy in the back yelled, "Look at that weirdo just standing there!"

"Sit down, asshole!" another yelled.

Holding back tears, I didn't know what to do or where to go, standing like I was on stage in the front of the bus. Someone decided to throw something at me, and it whizzed past my ear, causing the bus driver to yell at me.

"Young man, find a seat right now!" the older male driver hollered with his head cocked at a weird angle, looking at me in the mirror.

Nobody wanted to give me a seat, and my fear froze me. What was I going to do?

The saga continued as I tried to walk forward, with backpacks thrown into empty seats, kids scooting over so I could not sit, and kids pushing or pulling my old red JanSport backpack down. The backpack was Reata's, and it smelled like charcoal and paint. I didn't care how old it was.

What was only thirty seconds of horrible bullying ended when a girl in the middle row didn't push herself or backpack over. She was a red-haired girl who looked out the window, not registering I was there. I sat on the very edge of the seat, not taking my backpack off and sniffling back the tears that puddled around my eyes.

"Thank you," I whispered and put my head in my hands. The green bench seat was cold, and I still held my face in my hands.

The girl did not respond, but I felt her adjust in her seat to look toward me. There was no way I was going to make eye contact. The next step was getting off the bus without someone pushing me around.

Not expecting a silent exit, I prepared myself for the impending monsters who would laugh at me. This bus had seventh graders up to seniors, and Mesa was an unforgiving, violent school.

We made about six or seven more stops, until we turned onto Fairview Drive and headed toward the unknown. I had nobody to talk to, nobody to walk with, and no friends.

The Orange County Fairgrounds were across the street from Costa Mesa High School, and we used that side street to make the first stop. I had no idea what to do, until the bus driver honked his horn.

"Middle schoolers, this is your stop. Kindly make your way off my bus," he said with a mild British accent.

I was only pushed into one seat before jumping off the last stair of the bus and scurrying past the bigger kids. Following the girl I sat next to and a few others, I made my way toward the middle school entrance.

Looking back at the bus, it again stopped about one hundred yards ahead and let off the high school kids at the main entrance of the school. Hopefully, I would not have to go over there for a few years. That was not the case.

I had to go there on the first day.

All the seventh graders had to meet in the band room for school orientation, and the first thing I noticed was all the security. They looked like off-duty police, and some were sitting in golf carts, watching us closely. I was with a group of Asian kids who could care less about me, and I sat quietly near the front.

The first bell rang, and a lady holding a microphone walked up to the front to introduce herself as the vice principal. I could tell right away the kids around me were uncaring and loud, as we could barely hear the principal above their obnoxious ranting.

"Please be quiet so you can get to your first class!" she said loudly, and it did nothing.

What was supposed to be my introduction to middle school

ended up with stern security guards booting everyone out and closing the band room. It was sudden chaos, and I had no idea where I was going.

Standing outside the band room, confused, I had no clue what to do. Everyone knew where they were going, and I froze in panic. Kids were friends here, and many of them were from other grade schools.

Before long, the security guards had focused on me, as I was the only one around, and I felt panic shake my body. I couldn't make my foot move, and embarrassment saturated my eyes.

Then someone spoke to me. "Hey, dude, you okay?" said a Korean kid with a strong accent, holding a tuba.

My fear subsided, and I said, "I just don't know where to go."

He looked at me for a second and then took the schedule I was holding.

"Didn't you go to orientation night last week?" he asked.

There it was. The group home was out of the loop on everything, and as long as the kid got on the bus, they were free from worry. "No, I didn't know there was one," I said, looking down.

"I have the same first-period history class and just need to drop off my tuba. Let's go together. I know where it is," he said.

I still wasn't sure if he was messing with me.

Half expecting him to leave me standing like a dumbass in the hallway, I started looking around, and the security guards had left. The bell rang, and I knew it meant the first period had started.

The other kid came running out and said, "Let's go, dude!"

He booked it upstairs, taking two steps at a time, and I could barely keep up. Thankfully, the class was the first room at the top of the stairs, and we ran in before the teacher closed the door.

"You boys are late!" she said but didn't pursue us.

There were two seats in the back next to each other, and we could not believe that just happened.

Laughing, the boy said, "Hey, my name is Sung Park. What is yours?"

"Uh, Jeremy Bracamontes," I said, giggling still. He didn't even make fun of my name.

With that chance encounter, I met my best friend, and I knew God was watching out for me. I wasn't alone, and we ended up having many of the same classes. He was new to the school, coming from Diamond Bar, and he didn't know anyone either.

It was either my third- or fourth-period math class I had without Sung that the bullies came out.

The only seat available in math was at the front. It was an introductory class Mesa made kids take who had not tested out in sixth grade. It was also the class where the gangsters, cholos, druggies, and degenerates congregated. The classroom itself was on the outskirts of the middle school area, near the sports fields.

"Sitting in the front like a little brownnosing bitch!" someone said to me, and I felt something hit the back of my head. Laughter came from all around me, and I would not look back. The teacher was not in the classroom yet, and I saw an empty can of soda roll past my backpack.

"Come on, say something, bitch," the same voice was right behind me, and I slithered farther into the desk, not knowing what to do. I was not a tough kid and way too emotional to act like I was.

He smacked the back of my head, getting more of a rise from

the class, and kicked my backpack toward the teacher's old wooden desk. He tried to pull me out of my seat, but I held on for dear life, until I fell over with it, smacking my head on the dirty tile floor.

The laughter went on as I tried to untangle myself, and when I looked up, the teacher was staring at me. "What happened, young man?"

Silence pulsated from the room of misfits, and I knew they expected me to rat on the boy who pushed me over. I still had no idea who he was.

"Nothing, sir, I fell over," I said quickly and remained silent until class was over.

I couldn't wait for the teacher to end class so I could run from my shame. There wasn't a moment I didn't hear snickering or laughter behind me. When the bell rang for the next class, I jumped out of the chair to run out but was stopped by a hand holding the back of my sweatshirt.

"You ain't so bad, fool," said a big Mexican kid who had the same voice as my culprit. "I won't fuck with you, since you didn't rat me out, fool."

He sauntered off in a huge group of homies, and I let out a sigh of relief. Keeping my mouth shut and being silent was going to get me through this.

After a few weeks of figuring out my schedule and classes, things fell into place at Mesa. The Traverse home was oblivious to life there and had no stakes in the success of me as a student. My rule was simple—get on the bus at school and get off the bus at my stop.

I was not allowed to play sports or stay after for recreational activities. There were no exceptions with sports, and if I missed the bus, they gave me the option to walk home, if I made it back around the same time as the drop-off. It was a long walk, but sometimes it was worth it to hang out with Sung for a bit by the school.

Sometimes we would walk across the street to Orange Coast Community College, but it was short-lived, as I had a time limit I couldn't break. The college had a diverse group of people, and it was easy to walk around the campus. As long as it wasn't during class hours, or the security would catch us.

Sung lived in the opposite direction off Harbor Boulevard, at the Mediterranean Apartments closer to the back side of OCC. If I stayed after school, I would have to walk home alone fast, and it was hard to avoid thuggish neighborhoods, where I could get jumped. This happened more than once, but one occasion scared the life out of me.

I wasn't supposed to cut through the Marshall Islander territory, as they hated everyone who was not from their culture. I had no choice on this day. I had stayed too late hanging out with Sung and eating his dad's Korean pastries.

I ran through the Mesa football field and tried to sneak through their ominous street.

I passed the OG laundromat, where people bought weed all the time and played a few arcade games. My pace slowed, thinking I had made it clear, and I slithered through the shadows of the old palm trees. Almost to Baker Street, I had only one area to get through, and the coast was clear.

Two huge islanders turned the corner and zeroed in on me. I

was not allowed to be here. They knew it, and I knew it.

Cursing under my breath, I kept my head down and tried to walk on the grass, staying out of their way. Those big boys made sure to walk in my path. I felt fear take over my body. I knew how bad they beat up outsiders who trespassed.

"What are you doing here, white boy?" the bigger of the giants asked without asking.

"Why the fuck are you here, homie?" It was a statement from the other guy, not a question.

"I am sorry. I am just trying to get home," I stuttered miserably.

"Too late for that, bitch, but we won't beat your ass if you have twenty bones," the other teenager said, laughing, knowing I wouldn't have it.

My grandpa had given me ten dollars the last weekend, and I had five left. I had planned to buy myself a Caramello and a Slush Puppie at the Circle K by the group home, but hoped it would be enough.

Still shaking and keeping my head down, I handed them my five-dollar bill and said, "This is all I have. You can check—I swear."

Swiping the money from my hands, they pushed me into the brick planter around one of the palm trees, laughing. "We should kick your ass for being such a pussy," the bigger kid said.

The other boy kicked me in the ribs, hard enough to knock the wind out of my lungs, and laughed. "You better never come by our hood again, faggot."

I heard them laughing at me as they walked away, and I could not hold back tears. I should never have cut through that neighborhood.

Sitting there with my head down and holding my ribs, I didn't say anything. Tears spilled down my face, and I didn't want them to see how humiliated I was. Both my elbows were scratched up, and my wrists ached from trying to catch my fall.

The smell of grass and dirt enveloped me, and the sun peaked through the thick blades of the palm trees, creating long lines of light. No cars were around, and not a soul could be seen. People were watching from their windows, hidden behind curtains or blinds.

Long shadows pulled away from the judging trees and houses, which reminded me that time was running out. I knew better than to walk through their territory, and I got what I deserved. Both those high school–aged boys had dropped out of Mesa and were probably working for their family business.

Collecting myself, I rushed toward Baker Street and almost ran the rest of the way to the group home. On the way there, I tried to wipe off the dirt and scratches on my arms. My ribs hurt, but at least they didn't punch me in the face.

Across the street from the Circle K, by the Traverse House, was a local fish taco restaurant called Wahoo's, and I loved the intoxicating aromas emanating from that place. I never had the money to eat there.

"Jeremy, what have you been up to? You look like you got into a fight," Rebecca said as I walked in.

"I am sorry. I wasn't paying attention walking home, fell down that little hill by the bus stop, and rolled into that big pine tree. I am sorry I am late, Rebecca," I said pathetically.

There was no way I was telling them I got jumped for the rest of my money. I would just tell Grandpa I used it to buy my slushy and chocolate. Rebecca looked at me suspiciously, but I never got into trouble. She believed me.

I never walked the Marshallese path again and used Tewinkle Park to walk to the baseball field. The Costa Mesa Police gang unit had stakeouts there and loved to bust kids smoking or dealing dope during school hours. I would take that berating interrogation any day instead of getting jumped.

Living poor in group homes around Costa Mesa was hard. I felt like I was destined for failure. I saw the group home kids who ran away to join gangs, and I was not one of them. I would never join a gang, even if sometimes I thought it was easier.

I never told my grandpa how horrible Mesa was.

June 3rd.

Dear Jeremy,

How IF U ?!? Well, You know I

CAME BY TO VISIT U... BUT U WERE ON

A [school] (SCHOOL) TRIP... I MISSED NOT

SEEING U ON [sun]-DAY. TOMORROW I'M

GOING OUT OF [town] (TOWN) 4 A WEEK.

WHEN [eye] GET BACK I'M [back on] TO

THE BIG [apple] (APPLE) NEW YORK. I

HAVE TO [bee] (BEE) BACK IN NEW YORK

FOR WORK. SO U SEE I HAVE

A PROBLEM... I WANT TO SEE YOU

AND I DON'T HAVE THE [clock] (TIME).

SO WHAT AM I TO DO... WELL JER

I'M SO SORRY ☹ I MISSED. HERE IS

MY ADDRESS IN N.Y. - AND MY PHONE #

CALL ME... RENTA SEALS, 29 CASTLE PLACE

NEW ROCHELLE, N.Y. 10805

OVER ☆

CHAPTER 21

MAGIC

Costa Mesa, California, 1993

Of all possessions a friend is the most precious.
—HERODOTUS

Limp, trampled grass and trash were everywhere below the balcony everyone spat off. High school boys would hang out up top, showing off for girls by hurling bottles at poor middle schoolers caught in the open. The target was always a gleeful headshot to them.

I learned the hard way on a few occasions.

If I stayed close to the lockers and got to class quickly, I escaped being thrown out into the open by the older kids. Small kids who walked alone were easy targets.

I was shoved out past the sidewalk and slid into the dirty brown grass, in full view of the spit snipers upstairs. At the same time, milk was poured on me. I tried to get up and run farther out of range, but the damage had been done. The laughter was loud, and I didn't bother looking up at all the kids pointing at me. I felt it.

Spending the day smelling like old milk was as bad as trying to run to the bathroom to wash off spit in my hair. Laughter from all around me stung. Not a single person cared about the group home kid.

Sung and I hung out almost every day, but he was not around when I was bullied. He had been accepted into the marching band, and that changed many of our shared classes throughout middle school. That gave me a lot of time alone and more time to hide from the mean kids.

At lunch, we would meet up most days. His dad would make him a Korean-style lunch, and I was always jealous. I at least was able to eat school lunch without worrying where the food or money came from.

None of the homies messed with me in that line. They realized I was just like them, struggling and not in that group of privileged kids. A daily reminder of not having money was smelling the lucky kid's Pizza Hut or Taco Bell. We sat away from the main tables outside, around old brick planter beds, but the smell of delicious fast food was never far.

There were sects at Mesa. Gangs from every ethnicity had carved out pieces of the school, which became their turf. It was smart to steer clear.

Smart students, who were also the cool kids or athlete groups, took over the rest of the area, and we were not allowed around them. The athletes were aggressive, unless the other kids were in sports. The gangsters had their own cliques, and so did the rich kids.

Chaos danced around us middle schoolers, and the central

lunch area was a free-for-all. Fights broke out every day, and we learned quickly to stay in the shadows or near the roving security guards. Sometimes we would witness a kid getting jumped into one of the many gangs past the main parking lot and could hear the spectators from far away.

After lunch, on one particular day, I had an appointment with the school guidance counselor to talk about how my classes were going. I had to walk through part of the high school to get to the administrator's office, and it was dangerous being alone. It was a day that molded my life forever.

●●●

Cold cement walls lined the pathway from the lunch area to the administration offices inside. To get there, a student had to walk past classrooms that lined up horizontally with lockers, along the walls between the entryways. The windows were in the back of the class and had frosted glass panels to stop kids from looking out.

One hallway gave way to both the library and where administrators had their offices. The only separation was a big hallway, sloping downward toward the middle school area. That was a long way off and the opposite exit.

The cinder block walls had long, thin windows that showed off the library but looked medieval. It was isolated and a common place to get jumped. I avoided this area as much as possible and walked around to make sure.

The back entrance of the high school was close to where my guidance counselor sat, and I thought I could sneak in without abuse. I found a spot to peek around the corner, and my heart sank. A group of thugs were blocking the doors and listening to loud rap.

Some jerk student pushed me into the corridor, and the thugs standing around looked at me like hungry hyenas. "What do we have here, fools?" one of the big kids said, walking toward me swiftly.

I ran the other way as fast as I could, which was not fast. Not toward the doors and my appointment but right at the only open area with grass on the left side. It was my only escape, and I didn't want a beatdown. I was not a fast runner, but that element of surprise gave me a small lead they followed.

I made it to the end of the school building, which was about one hundred yards away, and cut around a corner. There were a few lingering kids, but for the most part, everyone, but my pursuers, was walking to class.

"Get back here, you little faggot!" I heard one yell behind me.

I kept running and made it to the opposite entrance on the middle school side. It led back toward the administration offices. I could see the library on the other end, and the final chase began.

Old metal double doors swung open smoothly, but I got shoved hard from behind. I slid roughly on the old carpet and fell forward as the ground sloped down.

I flipped over myself painfully and landed on my feet.

This lucky maneuver gave me a few yards to run away from the yelling pursuers, and I felt the tears streaming in my eyes. People saw me get picked on, but no one stopped it. It was the way of things.

Ahead of me on the right was the hallway to the guidance

counselor, but I was not going to make it. I was just too small and too damn slow.

Miraculously, the big wooden doors to the library were open. I had to get in there.

Sliding along the carpeted floor, I made it through the doors, only to find two more doors, which I pulled open quickly. I looked back quickly, knowing those thugs would not be following me, and I could see them pointing at me. They were throwing up gang signs and sliding their fingers across their necks.

I had to hide.

Turning around, I tripped over the dull silver turnstile and made a ruckus but was going to hide there for as long as I had to. I landed hard on my knee and ran to the right, passing a huge island that had magazines and newspapers hanging off it.

"Hey, young man, you can't do that!" I heard a female voice say behind me.

Ignoring her, I turned to see if the pursuers had followed me and ran straight into a solid wood bookshelf. My shoulder hit the corner so hard books fell everywhere, and I landed on my butt. Nobody followed me.

Time stopped before me.

My hand pushed away from the one book that landed in my lap. The cover had a red monster with the tail of a scorpion and the body of a lion. That beast was a manticore, and I was enthralled. A huge castle gate was drawn behind it and left me wondering what this book could be about. There was a man looking up at the manticore in defiance.

The author, Piers Anthony, had his name displayed vividly over the top. The title, *A Spell for Chameleon*, was in even bigger letters above the castle gate, and I was captivated. Reading was something smart people did.

A few seconds passed before I felt a presence above me. The librarian was there. Silence fled behind her, and she smiled at me with brilliant white teeth.

"Are you okay?" she asked, concerned.

Tears were still on my cheeks, and I was shivering. Maybe she was just trying to figure out what happened. I didn't want to tell her. "I am okay, and I am really sorry for making this mess," I said, looking around with my hand out.

Books littered the floor around me. I could see a few kids in the background staring at me, and the book I was holding felt heavy in my hands. My backpack was half off my arm, and I felt horrible for making a scene in her library.

The manticore was staring back up at me, and I knew I had to open the book.

"Do you like fantasy books?" the librarian asked.

"Like with dragons and stuff? I guess so," I said and opened the book, still sitting on the ground. An ornately drawn map with a north arrow drew me in. The world must have been called Xanth, as it was written in the middle of the map. Time stopped again.

She didn't say anything as I read the first page. Or the second. She didn't say anything at all for a long time. It started with the main character, who was shunned by those around him for being different. I related immediately.

Something connected within my mind, and I felt at peace. I felt the words on the paper and imagined them exactly as my mind read them. The characters came to life before me, and I in turn became them as the story moved on. I was the main character.

The librarian had left, and I was still sitting on the floor. I was also already on the second chapter of the book. She must have cleaned up the other books, as everything had been put back in its place.

I could hear a distant keyboard clicking away. None of the kids were there, and I was alone with my book. I was already cleared from my class, but not where I was supposed to be.

My appointment with the counselor had passed, but the librarian saw what had happened. I hoped the bullies were not lurking around the school, waiting for me.

Would the librarian give me a pass to get out of being tardy?

I walked over to the front desk, which was littered with old books, both hard and paperback. Old Apple Macintosh computers hummed gently to the right of the desk, near the newspaper and magazine area. I waited for the librarian to notice me in her office, behind the counter.

She got up slowly and walked over to where I stood with a smile on her face. "Found a book you like, I see?"

Smiling back, I said, "Yes, I can't stop reading it!"

"Piers Anthony is an amazing fantasy author. He is like Asimov to the science-fiction genre. You found the first book in his Xanth series. What is your name, young man?"

"Jeremy," I said back.

I had read a bit about the world of Xanth and could not wait to read more. Looking at the clock, I realized I was going to miss my bus if I didn't hurry.

"I am sorry. I have to catch my bus, but can I take this book, please?"

She asked me for the library card in the back and to put my last name on it. I did that and started to read as I walked out. No jackers in sight, and she gave me a pass.

"Make sure to look up, and don't run into anything," I heard her say as I walked out the door and made my way to the bus stop.

It was a day I would never forget.

What turned out to be a terrible experience and barely avoiding getting beat up became life-changing. Magic filled my life and a void I never knew existed. The loneliness and isolation in the group homes would soon disappear, like the magic in which I was reading.

Magic—it was real to me. I read that book on the bus, all the way home from the bus stop to the house, and over dinner. It was impossible to put down, and I couldn't stop.

I read that entire book in one day. Sitting on the old couch in the living room, after dinner that day, I read and read. At night, when we were supposed to be asleep, I had a flashlight, reading under my covers. It was glorious.

I fell asleep with that book next to me in bed. Before going to my first class the next day, I went to the library. The sweet librarian had already put aside the next two books in the series for me.

When she saw me walking in before class, a big smile came across her face, and she said, "You finished the book, didn't you, Jeremy?"

"How did you know?" I asked, smiling back.

"I could tell right away you were a reader once you opened

that book!" she said.

"These are the next two books in the series, and I already ordered the next five since our library needed them, and I know you will be finished fast," she said smartly.

"Thank you so much. That really is nice of you," I said softly and felt tears in my eyes. These books gave me access to a whole new world and a way out.

A way out of group homes, even if it wasn't real.

"Come by in a few days to get the other books and drop off those two," she said with her hand out. I had to give back *A Spell for Chameleon*. For some strange reason, I really wanted to keep it.

"Okay, I will!" I said happily, skipping back out to my first period.

"Oh, try this book. I have a feeling you might like it too," she said, sliding it over. The book was *The Sword of Shannara*, by Terry Brooks.

Holding those books in my arms felt right. The power that was given to me allowed me freedom and love. I never thought I could feel that way about something like reading.

I shivered with excitement and put all the books away, except for the second Xanth novel. It was called *The Source of Magic*, and the cover was even more beautiful than *A Spell for Chameleon*.

A huge dragon towered over a centaur holding a bow and the main character, Bink, holding a large magical sword. Every character in the book had a magic talent, but Bink's talent was hidden and not identified until the end. His magician-level talent was the power to be immune to all magic, and he had to use it to save Xanth.

Thus began my eternal love affair with books, reading, and finding true happiness in a creative mind.

Middle school became a game of how many books I could read a week. My grandpa loved it, and we would sit all day reading books together in his den with golf in the background. I was blessed.

CHAPTER 22

FRESHMAN

Costa Mesa High School, 1994

Science fiction frees you to go anyplace and examine anything.
—OCTAVIA BUTLER

Mystical realms consumed me. I read everything in the library fantasy section and went for the biggest books that were in a series first. If the school didn't have it, I scoured the public libraries. My grandfather loved my passion for reading, and we spent the weekends reading through our books.

Bella made me pasta or amazing tacos with fried-up corn tortillas that melted in my mouth every weekend. I loved her cooking. They allowed me a small glass of wine at dinner, and Grandpa always took me to Arby's for lunch.

The weekend sanctuary at my grandpa's gave me enough to pretend the week at the Traverse home was just a pit stop into my real life with the Butler family. Most weekends his sons and grandkids would show up to have Saturday or Sunday dinner. We would play cards after, or all the grandkids would watch movies.

They let us use the paddleboat out back and roam around the neighborhoods together. It was wonderful and made time fly.

I was still the only original Traverse kid left, besides Peter, and I was given extra freedoms around the neighborhood. Peter was spending more time in the developmentally disabled home, as his seizures became increasingly violent. Sometimes a friend from school, who lived close by, would invite me to hang out, and I could walk over, but it was embarrassing.

Their parents had to sign a form that said they would be responsible for me during my time away from the home, and most times I would not accept those invitations.

In SoCal high school, house parties were life. This was where deep friendships formed, girlfriends found, and experiences remembered for a lifetime. Parties near the beach, in nice bungalow homes and even at the top of some obscure parking lot, were the talk of the week when something was planned.

I never went. Nobody told me where the parties were. I expected it, but the feeling of isolation equaled the sadness in being left behind again. No matter how kind and happy I was as a person, it didn't matter.

By ninth grade, nobody knew me outside the school. In school, I bonded more with teachers.

Listening to everyone planning to go to these parties, talking about it, and all the cool things they did taught me about isolation. Friendships became closer, and bonds were formed right in front of me, but I was invisible.

The group home didn't allow me to play sports, and even though I was small, I was athletic. They did not allow any form of school sport that caused us to be away from the home during hours the state mandated as "monitored."

Kids became popular as they went to more parties or could go to school booster events. I was never allowed to go to football games, and the only way I could go to a school dance was if one of the staff members chaperoned. That never happened.

My freshman year gave way to true loneliness. It taught me something else within a resilient fortitude—finding happiness with my own company.

I loved my books and read every single day, but it was impossible to not see everything around me. There was not a group of friends I could join, and nobody cared about that. Even Sung, my best friend, started hanging out with a cool group of Cambodian kids.

There was no way I could be mad at him, as he made sure to spend time with me, and I was still allowed to go to his parents' house once a week to have dinner with them. They signed the form first and were a lovely Korean couple who taught me their culture freely.

Sung had freedom, and to see him become popular from where he came from, back in seventh grade, made me happy.

This was not to say I was not popular, but I didn't have a place. Everyone knew me and liked me, but I was not "in." I was outgoing, talkative, and did well in school. I was a bookworm and proud of it.

In high school, gangs were a real thing and dangerous. I learned quickly even I couldn't wear certain colors. Fights broke out daily for wrong colors, and high school kids got hurt. They would get jumped in the parking lot or the church behind Mesa, and it was common to see kids with busted-up faces the next day.

I never got in fights, but I always got picked on, and it was insurmountably worse as a freshman.

Boys became young men quickly and had something to prove. They loved to show off in front of the pretty girls or their homies. My life quickly became a game of avoidance. Some things were unavoidable if the thugs were set on hurting me.

Moments of extraordinary fear loomed before me during breaks between class, lunch, and after school, due to the love bullies found in tormenting me. At this age, they were merciless on my small height, my physical immaturity, and my happy demeanor.

Finding power in a display of humiliation comprised much of my high school time, but it was the worst during freshman year. A day didn't go by when I left the group home that I didn't think about running away or even joining a gang and walking the easier path.

The girls were just as bad. If they were in the popular group, they laughed and said cruel or embarrassing things that everyone heard. It was easy to do.

On one warm day in October, a couple of months into my torturous freshman year, I got beat up bad. I did not know which gang or group it was, but the opportunity was too hard for them to pass up. A small and fragile group home kid, walking toward the school bus stop with no one around.

"Look at this little bitch right here," said one of the kids, most likely the ringleader.

"Is he a girl or just a female midget?" another boy said while my back was turned.

They knew I was scared, and I didn't want to turn around so they would not see my fear or my shaking body. They surrounded me, and malevolent intent was on their minds.

Stuttering, I said, "Just leave me alone."

They didn't. The kid who spoke first dropped his backpack and walked around so I could see him in front of me with balled-up fists. I had seen him before. He was not a big kid, but bigger than me, and he liked that. His smile was carnal and lopsided.

The reason he was smiling was that another boy had sneaked up behind me to grab me. He was big enough that my head was near his chest, and he squeezed me so my arms got stuck. I tried to wiggle out and hang my weight down, but the next thing I remembered was intense pain along the side of my head.

Nobody was around this area, and those few who walked by ignored us so they would not be targeted. My head hurt, and I felt queasy. It was hard to see anything but a blur, and that's when the guy holding me dropped me to the ground.

Hitting the ground hard was the starting point for those assholes to kick me. I felt my ribs go numb, and my head bounced around as they laughed. This was just a joke to these wannabe gangsters, or it was an initiation into their gang.

Covering my head and trying to roll into a protective ball helped hide my face, but my head was a soccer ball. They kept kicking the same ribs over and over. Then silence followed.

The boys had disappeared with their laughter and menace. Looking around, other kids were staring at me, laughing, or snickering, and many had resigned looks. It was just another shitty day at Costa Mesa High School.

I felt a sharp pain on my right side and could tell my ribs were either bruised or broken. It was hard to breathe, and I tried to pretend as I got on the bus that nothing was wrong, even with dried blood on my face. My split lips felt fat and tasted metallic.

Once I got back to the group home and away from all the whispering on the bus, I went straight to the bathroom. Luckily, my face was not severely busted, but I had a few lumps on the side of my head and a split lower lip. When I lifted my shirt, I saw a huge bruise forming along my right rib cage.

It hurt badly. Everything was still in the right place, and nothing felt broken, but how could I really know? I was not going to tell the group home or anyone else. The last thing I needed was another jumping for being a rat.

The next morning the intense pain had subsided on my side, but when I looked at it, all I saw was black, purple, and blue, with a tint of red. My first period was PE, and there was no way I could hide the pain but would try.

Flag football for PE really meant tackle. What group did I get stuck in? The shirtless group, and I knew the teacher was going to see my bruise. He watched out for me during class and would ask questions.

I would lie.

He knew I was a group home kid who got tortured daily. I had no choice and took my shirt off. If I just kept my head down, I hoped nobody would see.

"What the fuck happened to you, homie?" I heard a kid say to my right, and he seemed genuinely concerned.

His name was Dennis Gomes, and he was a solidly built guy who I knew took no shit from anyone. I had seen him around the school before, with some other tough guys, and tried to stay away so I wouldn't get beat up. We would end up becoming close friends instead.

"That looks fucked up, man!" said Ronnie Sou, a cool Cambodian who was friends with Dennis.

They both walked over to me and made me lift up my arm. It was embarrassing, but I could tell when Dennis looked at me that he knew what happened or had heard.

"Jeremy, are you okay? Did you get beat up again?" the teacher asked, as he heard the commotion and all the kids around me looking at the nasty bruise that took up my whole side.

"Uh, no, Coach, I just fell when I got out of the shower and hit the side of the tub," I said quickly before he could push for more information.

Dennis and Ronnie looked at me with a smirk. They knew I was not a snitch.

An epic beatdown became the catalyst for what changed my lonely life forever. Dennis and Ronnie became real friends and were also homies with Sung, so that connected us again. They asked if I could hang out after school, and as I started to feel embarrassed, Dennis put his hand on my shoulder, saying, "It doesn't matter. We can just ditch during the day."

I had never ditched before, and I had never hung out with other kids far from the group home. My naivety was paramount, and it showed by my stupid smiling face. "Bro, you can't always be smiling like that, or people will keep picking on you," Ronnie said, laughing.

I tried to not smile so openly, but it was difficult. I couldn't believe these cool guys were even talking to me. I finished up PE and ditched with them the rest of the day at Dennis's house, not far from the school.

There was a whole group of kids who hung out there, and his lovely mom didn't care as long as we stayed nearby. Noreen was the sweetest woman I had ever met outside Reata. She felt terrible for me living in group homes and told Dennis that he better not let anything else happen to me.

Noreen mothered me, fed me, and loved me. I could not believe how lucky I was again to have that attention. Dennis and his mother helped me through a time I thought would never get better.

Everyone smoked cigarettes, but I had never tried and didn't want to. My grandpa and Bella smoked, but they were from another generation. They smoked so much inside that the walls of their home had a shade of yellow stained on them.

I knew, though, that to be cool, I had to try it.

I asked Sung one morning to ditch with me to Tewinkle Park so that I could see what this was all about. He was hesitant at first, but I insisted and had to practically beg for a cigarette. I knew there was no going back at this point, but what else did I have to do?

Sung smoked Marlboro Reds, and I remember sitting on the bench as he showed me how to light it with a small black Bic lighter. I looked like a child.

My lungs imploded. I had a hard time standing from the

coughing and dizziness. Immediately, I lay down on the damp picnic table, with my head hanging over. I felt ill and stupid.

Sung just laughed his ass off and told me, "I told you, fool. This shit is no joke."

I looked at him with both anger and humor. We ditched school the rest of the day, and I even tried another "square" once my nausea subsided.

That was the day I smoked with my best friend and started making wrong choices. At least my grandpa and grandma smoked, so they would not smell it on me.

I would test that out on the weekends I went to visit and stole a few squares from my gramps. He loved Marlboro Reds, too, and left them out on the table. When we went to Costco together on Sundays to try all the free food they handed out, he would also grab a couple of cartons for himself as well as the Virginia Slims for Bella.

When South Coast Children Society moved me out of Traverse to an emancipation home called the Dahlia house, it became a lot easier to "want" to bad.

My freedom and reign at Traverse were over.

CHAPTER 23

EMANCIPATION

Costa Mesa, 1995

———————

No act of kindness, no matter how small, is ever wasted.
—AESOP

Steely clouds were heavy in the sky, and I could smell rain in the dense air. I got off the bus smelling like an ashtray. I was chewing gum, so if I could get to my room at the Traverse house before anyone got close, things would be okay.

They were not. I walked in, and people were waiting for me.

The Saint and Kathy were sitting at the dining-room table with Rebecca. They all stood up when I walked in, and in desperation I grabbed my stomach while running to the bathroom. I apologized as I ran toward a quick escape, "Sorry, I have to go bad."

I took my hoodie off and used the last of the Scope in the bottle. I washed my hands multiple times and then my face, hoping the smell of cigarettes was gone.

I sprayed the air with Lysol and walked under the blast as a last resort.

The smell of Lysol and cigarettes reminded me of Las Vegas nickel arcades inside the old Riviera. Bill, Grandpa's son, invited me with Big Frank and their kids to the land of casinos a few years back. We drove with Frank and his old police partner in a weathered camper van. I never knew how much Bella loved her slot machines until that trip. I read books the whole way, and Bill even bought me a Super Soaker to play with his sons.

I usually gave the Saint a big hug, but this time I shook his hand. A little surprised at my action, the Saint smiled and gave me a big shake in return. "Jeremy, how are you, buddy?"

Feeling ashamed of my smoking earlier, I said, "I am good and ready to stop being a freshman. It's brutal out there."

He just laughed and said, "It's almost over, and that is why we are here. Can you sit with us, please?"

Seeing him so somber brought a bit of dread to my spine, and my queasiness came back. He saw my face—probably the fear—and knew I thought Orangewood. I sat down close to the window at the kitchen table next to Kathy, who patted my knee.

Something was wrong. "Am I in trouble?" I asked.

"Oh, Jeremy, not at all, but we have some very important news to share with you, and I hope you can understand the situation," Kathy said before the Saint could chime in.

An awkward moment of silence led to Bob clearing his throat and saying, "Jeremy, first I wanted to thank you for making the Traverse house a wonderful place to be, and you have been the best role model for all the kids who have come through here."

Smiling, I just nodded as the fear crept up to my neck. Rebecca had her head lowered a bit and I could tell she was sad.

"Are you sending me back to Orangewood?" I asked softly.

"Never, Jeremy. We would never do that, but you are going to have to move to the Dahlia house, where Ramon is. He is one of your best friends, right?" the Saint asked.

I was silent, looking down at my hands on the table, and mumbled a miserable, "Yes."

The pain of leaving hit me hard.

This place had been my home for almost eight years, and I was the oldest. I had more freedom and could visit friends in nearby homes. Was all this going away?

Ramon told me at Dahlia, all the staff members, besides Becky, were horrible. He had no freedom and hated how they treated him. He was a great friend, who always looked out for me at school when he could.

Ramon was a big guy who took no shit and made sure people knew I was his homie. This didn't stop the beatdowns or getting jumped, but I am sure it made a few bullies think twice. I appreciated that more than Ramon could ever know.

Looking up while trying to remain confident was difficult, but I said, "I understand and thought this was going to happen sooner anyway."

The Saint looked at me thoughtfully and said, "Well, buddy, can we do this today?"

A little shocked, I cocked my head, and before I could say anything, the Saint continued, "There is a young boy at Orangewood we would love to get out of there. He is in a similar situation you were in, remember?"

Bob Ford knew my weak points.

"Really? Let's get him out of there!" I said.

Kathy and the Saint looked over at Rebecca, who had tears in her eyes. I had forgotten about her, as she was silent, and realized how hurt she was. She was a sweet woman who really cared about me, and I was leaving.

I ran over, not caring about smoke smells, and hugged her fiercely.

We both cried, and it felt good to close things that way with her. When she let me go, there was a smile on her face, and she whispered to me, "Jeremy, you keep being you, and never ever let anyone take your happiness. It is your strength and what draws people to you. Use it for good."

I will always remember her words and said them over and over to myself as I packed my stuff.

The Saint and Kathy were in the van, but Rebecca was by the door, waiting for me with Keith. They both gave me hugs and said they would miss me as I tried to leave quickly before the flood of emotions took over.

The Saint had leased a new vehicle. He told me all the time: leasing was better than buying. I had no clue what he was talking about. When I got in the car, he asked about my part-time job working at a mortgage firm as the office gopher.

Six months before my departure from Traverse, I was given the opportunity to participate in a state-run program for wards of the court who excelled in the system. I was a good kid who did what was right, most of the time.

That program allowed the kid, after a formal interview, to work part-time at companies who wanted to help, and one of those was a mortgage firm in Newport Beach. I worked three days a week after school and took the bus out in front of the high school. It was freedom. I got paid, and it was nice being a part of something so important to those stuck in the homes.

I wanted to set a good example and learned early from my grandpa when scouting out movie locations that to be early is on time. I was at the worksite at least fifteen minutes early. My jovial attitude allowed me to run around and talk with everyone, but my primary job was to help with the mail.

In the car, the Saint let me know everything was good with the job, but that it was ending in a few months due to program requirements. "Jeremy, I have a friend who works at an office building near John Wayne Airport and needs an assistant. Can you help with that once you have completed your time with the current job?"

He spoke to me like an adult, and I immediately said, "Absolutely!"

That took the edge off the fear boiling in my stomach. The fear of a new place, having to make new friends, and wondering if I would be accepted.

Dahlia house was a massive home in Costa Mesa, not far from Traverse, and seemed inviting at the end of a cul-de-sac. Behind the house was a big parking structure with huge trees lining the side of the home at the end of the street.

A beautiful, young Hispanic woman with flowing curly black hair, who I assumed was Becky, waved out front happily, with Ramon next to her, smirking. Maybe it wouldn't be so bad.

CHAPTER 24

DAHLIA

Costa Mesa, California, 1995–1996

———

Loss is nothing else but change, and change is Nature's delight.
—MARCUS AURELIUS

The scent of engine oil and strawberries twisted together and danced toward me as I slowly walked toward Ramon, who said, "Órale, Jeremy! Finally here! This is Becky, homie."

Becky hugged me gently, while her hair fell around me like a cocoon, and I knew where that strawberry smell came from. I could see why Ramon loved her. She radiated kindness.

The front door opened quickly, and I sensed both Ramon and Becky stiffen. "Hey, Mr. Ford, so glad you came personally to drop off the new kid!" said the nasally voice.

Looking around the side of Becky to see who it was, Ramon grabbed my arm as a warning and slightly shook his head no. I made sure to remain silent. The man was a tall, balding white guy named Andy and, from what I was told, a tool.

His arrogance was noted by the Saint, who said, "Andy, he's

been with South Coast Children's Society for eight years and could probably teach you some things."

I cringed inside as Andy slowly turned his gaze toward me, and I saw the predatorial smirk that would get me into trouble soon. "Oh, I bet he can, Bob. Jeremy, why don't I show you to your room?" he said innocently.

Since this dude was going to target me anyway, I ignored him and walked over to the Saint and Kathy, giving them long hugs that only someone who knows them could do. They reciprocated, and Kathy said while getting in the passenger seat, "Hey, Jeremy, call us anytime. We are always here for you!"

Ramon was looking at me with shock, and Miss Strawberry was smiling. I walked toward them, looking at Andy in a way that made him hate me immediately. When he gestured for me to follow him, I asked, "Am I bunking with Ramon since we are such good friends?"

Andy remained silent for a moment and then said, "We can't have that in this house, now can we? Two troublemakers in one room."

Ramon mumbled, "*Puto*," which meant bitch.

"Drop your stuff in the room with the empty bed and get settled before we have dinner, Jeremy," Miss Strawberry said with a gentle push on my back toward the stairs.

Andy had forgotten about me and sat down in the living room across from the large kitchen in a comfy chair.

Walking up the wide, curving staircase, Ramon showed me to my room, which was next to his, and said, "Sorry, homie, I asked them to put us together, but Andy is a *pendejo*."

"It's cool, homie," I said, slapping hands.

I don't remember the kids in that home. They kept to themselves and were not interested in making a new friend. I couldn't blame them for that. My roommate was a big guy named George, who was almost eighteen and getting ready to emancipate.

Ramon and Big Cole, who went to Mesa as well, were roommates.

George was allowed to work after school at the local grocery store, so we barely saw him. My job was ending soon, and I was hoping the Saint could hook me up with his friend at the airport. Having my own money was nice, and he had helped me open a checking account that came with its own debit card.

A few days into my Dahlia imprisonment, things got bad.

I was in my room reading a Clive Cussler Dirk Pitt novel called *Dragon* when I heard yelling in the hallway outside. All the rooms were on the top floor, with a large, curved landing in the center used for tutoring that opened to the wooden stairs on the right. The house was big, and if it wasn't a group home, it probably would have been a wonderful place to live.

I peeked out the room and saw Ramon getting pushed into his room by Andy, who looked like he wanted to fight. Not a good idea with my boy there, so I ran over and tried to separate them. That was a bad idea.

Andy pushed me back hard, and I slid all the way to the staircase, falling over my body right to the railing. He looked back at what he did and smiled, forgetting about Ramon. "You okay there, little buddy? Need me to call your savior, Mr. Ford?"

Ramon charged over and pushed him so hard he lost his footing and stumbled right into me. Instead of catching him, I moved out of the way, and that made Andy fall right down the stairs.

He hit his head hard on the second landing and looked up at us with the craziest eyes I had ever seen. At the base of the stairs, Miss Strawberry looked up in disbelief and had a phone in her hand, which I believe she was going to use to call the police.

"What is going on? Andy, are you okay?" she asked.

He looked right at me and grinned with evil passion and said, "Jeremy, you just lost all your privileges, and you can kiss any free time goodbye."

I was devastated, but looking back at Ramon, who was silently laughing in his doorway, I knew it was all worth it.

Tool was his name. All the kids came by my room at different times to laugh with me about the situation. That guy had it coming and constantly taunted Ramon, who had never done anything. We were inseparable at the home, but during school he was located with the ESL students.

The bus stop was far from our house, but all us boys going together as a group was fun, and I knew some of them would not let me get beat up in the new neighborhood. This was the little freedom we had, and I could not understand why the Dahlia house had failed to prepare us for life on the outside.

Some of the kids were a flight risk, but none were being taught how to survive in the real world, and that was why gangs were so enticing. A few of the boys were already in a gang, but I never said a word about that and acted like I had no idea. I gained their trust, and at school I was not targeted by those who had used me as a punching bag.

It was refreshing not getting beat up or targeted.

Dahlia home had some tough dudes living there, and I made sure to stay out of their way. My books saved me, and most of them thought I was a small, harmless nerd. I guess I was, and that was okay.

My grandfather would come to see me on the weekends, but it changed to only a couple of times a month, and many times I could not stay the night. His kidneys had started failing, and that meant on most Saturdays he went to dialysis in Newport Beach. At first he was embarrassed when I begged him to come to hang out at the nephrology clinic, but he soon realized he needed me just as much.

Those weekends were hard.

He got worse but never showed it and always drove himself, telling me, "It's just like going to get this rig an oil change."

On those weekends, I would go with him to dialysis and read next to him, and he did the same. It became a competition to see how far we could get in our books, and he let me win most times. I loved him so much; it hurt to see the doctors take him back in a hospital gown and wheelchair.

At least he could wear his regular pants underneath; they only needed his arms.

They would let me come visit once he was up and running, but I will never forget the first time I saw him connected to dialysis. Nurses would hand me gloves and a mask, and horrible memories hit me when that ether smell took over.

My dad and now my grandpa.

He was sitting up in a comfortable chair, with both arms laid out on the black-padded armrests. Tubes full of his blood ran from one arm to the revolving metal machine behind the chair and back into the other arm. Grandpa had monitoring devices all over him but could keep his arms close enough together to read.

Behind him, the dialysis apparatus looked like a slushy machine with a disk in the middle mixing his blood and cleaning it. The process took many hours, and I could tell how much it was hurting my grandpa. Learning how to act lighthearted in tough situations was difficult, but we would enjoy each other's company, until he was discharged.

Bella started coming with us to drive, and that is when I knew he was getting worse.

Grandpa never complained and acted like things were okay, but his movements became much slower. He walked slow and hunched over more but still had that glorious mane of perfect silver hair. His deep voice still held strength, and as a joke, he started using me as a walking stick.

Getting home took a while from Newport Beach to Huntington Beach, and he would often fall asleep in the back of their big caddy. Bella would ask me to sit up front to keep her company, and she was so sweet. I would do anything for her. She was hurting from this and hated seeing her husband of over fifty years wounded, not getting better.

We spent a lot of weekends, just the three of us. Sometimes their kids or grandkids showed up, but mostly I was their constant companion from Friday night to Sunday night. Sometimes I would stay until Monday morning, if my grandpa was too weak to drive.

The Tool could not take that away, even if he wanted to.

One morning, after helping my grandpa into the back seat of the Fleetwood, I noticed a lot of bruising all over his arms, and his fatigue was worse than normal. His skin looked like it could rip apart just from touch. He just smiled at me as I closed the door, and by the time Bella started driving away, he was fast asleep.

The lack of sleep, his inability to clean his own blood, and still smoking cigarettes were causing havoc throughout his body. His skin was having trouble staying healthy and ripped easily. Grandpa soon started wearing long-sleeve shirts and not his normal short-sleeve button-ups he was so well-known for.

I did everything possible to ease his discomfort. We would watch golf all weekend, record movies to see later in the night, and I would keep his glass of vodka full. I loved him so much; seeing him hide pain was too much to bear.

Due to his declining health, Bella or one of her children, mostly Maria, began driving me to the Dahlia house after dinner on Sundays. The kids and grandkids were spending a lot more time over there, and even though I was beloved by Grandpa, I was not blood. I felt a bit like an outsider.

I made it through ninth grade at the Dahlia house in silence. The world around me warmed up to perfect temperatures, and I spent many days lounging in the backyard reading while the other kids threw a football or something. Miss Strawberry was working on her master's degree at Cal State, Fullerton, and would join me with her psychology textbooks in temporary solitude.

I also focused on going to the gym with Ramon, who was an elite runner, and some of the other boys. He jogged at my full-speed sprint, and I realized quickly my body was not made for running. Quick feet allowed me to play basketball and do martial arts well, but football—not a chance.

One day, during the summer of 1995, our psychologist at the time, Paul, rushed into the locker room to collect us group home kids. He was a fantastic tennis player and would decimate us on the court, but we loved the challenge anyway. On this day, back when people wore pagers on their pants, Paul got an emergency get-home code.

We had no idea what was going on but knew it couldn't be good. Our first thoughts were one of the other kids ran away or did something illegal, but it was far worse.

"Boys, when we get home, don't say anything until we know what has happened," Paul said dramatically. We lived only a couple of miles away from the gym, so we got there in just a few minutes.

Driving up in his black SUV, we saw Kathy's Lincoln Town Car and knew something was wrong. We sped into the house, feeling the stark silence and loud whispers. Kathy was talking to Becky, with tears in her eyes, while the Tool had the other kids in the large two-story family room.

Something terrible had happened, and it was obvious from the pain emitting from Kathy.

Once we were all seated in the living room on couches and on the floor, Kathy walked over in a shaky pattern and tried to speak. "Uh, boys, we have some terrible news about Bob Ford."

She couldn't continue for a minute while collecting herself, and Becky came over to help by guiding her toward an open chair. Kathy then said hauntingly, "Mr. Ford passed away this morning, and we are all very shocked by this tragedy, but we wanted you to be the first of the homes to know."

I looked at Ramon with tears welling up in my eyes and then started crying. The other boys didn't cry, but I could see the sadness on their faces. The Saint was always kind, open with his heart, and never said a negative thing to any of us. None of these boys knew him as I did, but he saved all of them from the streets.

We owed him, and the solemn vibe in the air spoke to that. I walked right up to Kathy and just hugged her. She was a great woman, who cared about helping kids who had nothing and never expected anything in return.

Something changed in me that day. I grew older and felt more of my innocence slip away. The weeks that followed were in memory of Bob, and all the group homes got together at the park near the Traverse house for a memorial. It was a good time with no restrictions.

Losing the Saint and seeing my grandpa deteriorate before my eyes stopped my happiness in its tracks.

Things slowly moved back to normal, and as we got closer to the start of the new school year, the Tool either quit or was let go. We were not sure, but it made our lives a lot easier. A new house-parent came in named Martha, and she was sweet.

She wore comfy sweaters with cat designs and was a close friend of our psychologist, Paul. He recommended her, and I believe he had a major part in Andy's removal. All the kids spoke of his vindictive actions.

Losing the Saint was very hard, and we rarely saw Kathy anymore, as she took charge of the company. It was a breath of fresh air having a kind houseparent. Miss Strawberry only worked weekends as my sophomore year started due to a residency for her school program and trying to move into clinical work.

My grandfather was maintaining a semblance of normalcy, but my weekends with him were shortened to just one day again, if that. Bella needed help from her kids to get him from dialysis to their home, and she didn't want me to see him in pain. It was hard to lose that time with him and not feel like a part of the family.

On most occasions, Maria would pick me up with one or two of her daughters, but some Sundays nobody would show up. I felt left out but tried to remain positive. That was a separation I had not felt in a long time, and I could not understand why I was being forgotten.

My path in life became skewed. My direction forward didn't move, and I felt my desire to do what was right slip away. In the span of a few months, I had lost what was my home for many years, one of my saviors, my freedom, and the chance to be there for my grandfather.

That path was no longer visible, and I found solace in something I vowed to stay away from: pot.

10-15-91

Jeremy

Hi Sweetheart! How are you
doing? I hope everything is going well.
I've been thinking about you so
much. I can't wait to see you, to
hug and kiss you. I hope you don't
feel your to old for some hugs from your
mom. It's going to be so wonderful.
It's been to long since we have
seen eachother.

It things work out like they
should I'll be leaving for the halfway house in a couple months. I'll
know for sure in a few weeks if
I have been accepted. So far things
look pretty good.

The past bothers me and
makes me feel very guilty. I just
can't look back at all the bad
stuff anymoe. The future is what
my life is all about now and
being able to make up for all all
the pain I caused you.

I never stopped loving you
honey, I've always loved you and
always will. Drug addiction is
a terrible thing. It took me from
you, but now I'm free from wanting
to get high. I just want to be
your mom Jeremy and to live

everyday to it's fullest. So many
years have passed. We have both
been cheated of precious time, time
that we should have been together.
I cherish every single moment we
shared. I look forward to each
new day because with every day
that goes by I get that much
closer to the day when I'll be
able to see you. You are my
little angel, my miracle, my son
(Forgive me Jeremy for)
(all the wrong I've done)

    I love you with all my heart
& Soul   forever

Honey I don't have any good
pictures but I sent you one
anyway —

              always,
              your mom

CHAPTER 25

ALLEY BOYS

Costa Mesa, Baker Street Alley, California, 1995–1996

━━━━━━━━━━━━

There is nothing on this earth more to be prized
than true friendship.
—THOMAS AQUINAS

Sung had gotten very close to Ronnie over the summer and into their own bad shit, but it was their world. I was not in a place to judge their choices, and Sung still made sure I was okay when he could. We would meet at his parents' apartment still, but it was either for lunch when we ditched or to go smoke weed in the apartment complex sauna.

That was always fun and smelled of cedar when we hit the bong. Most days, during school, I would be too preoccupied with ditching or hanging out with Dennis and that crew rather than my schoolwork. After the first-period photography class, we would leave school and take the bus to the beach, smoking joints while listening to the waves crash.

The school became a way to be with my friends, not to learn.

Most days we would sneak out the back of the school through an agricultural area so we could go to Dennis's house to smoke. This became a daily thing, and our crew got closer as the school year went on. My grades were average, at best, and I knew I could have done a lot better.

There was no one telling me about the repercussions of poor grades, the impossibility of college, and showing no discipline. Yet, as a group, we were the same and loved hanging out with each other.

The crew held no bias. We came from all walks of life, ethnicities, and struggles.

There was Dennis, who was a stocky guy of Brazilian and Irish descent, who was the glue of our group. His mother, Noreen, was the sweetest woman and an angel in her own right. She knew we were ditching but let us stay at the house rather than making trouble in the neighborhood. His stepdad, Big Marv, worked at Orange Coast College in the prosthetics department and was a wonderful man who loved Dennis and his brother, Little Marvin.

Pisa John was the pimp of our group and had the craziest stories. He was kind and a great friend. From early on, we knew he had something special.

Catfish was the one of the oldest brothers of the Mendez family and came from a line of cholos. He had a shaved head, mustache, and was an all-around gangster. Nobody fucked with Fish, and Dennis was his closest friend, which meant we were all family to him.

Peewee was a younger brother of Fish, and he followed the same path, dressed the same, and acted similarly but was still his own man. He was a great friend to have around and superprotective of our clique. Guppy was the youngest Mendez in our group, and where his older brothers went, he went.

Pierre was the biggest dude, in the best shape within our group, and loved by the cholas, but none could hold him down. He had a great sense of style and loved to talk shit or stir the pot. If we saw him running from something, it was most likely his cop sixth sense, and we went with him.

Mo was an awesome soul, who had a strong entrepreneurial spirit. He always had great ideas and wanted to try new things. He was a good person to have around and spoke his mind, even when it was in disagreement, which we all respected.

Ronnie would come by with his little brother, Rov, and they lived a couple of streets down. They always brought delicious Cambodian food to munch on. Both the brothers were fantastic football players, but Ronnie stopped playing to make other life choices. Rov and his best friend, Nick, would always be there with us to chill.

Nick was a tall and lovable guy, but no one wanted to piss him off. Besides Dennis and Fish, I was closest to Nick. He always looked out for me and reminded me all the time that just because I was a group home kid didn't mean I was any less than them.

As time went on, we would vet other homies to see if they were allowed into our family, but it was rare. At school, I felt like I had a place with them, and we did everything we could to share our money to buy enough herb for all of us to smoke.

We were the Alley Boys.

Everything revolved around not being in the shitty reality I lived in at the group home. If I could be high and with my buddies, nothing else mattered. Conquering the darkness of that group home gave me enough resolve to push toward the next day.

One day at a time.

There were some days it was especially hard. Waking up in the group home, knowing the coming weekend was going to be without my grandpa, and not knowing if he was okay, was unbearable. I missed everything about them—their home, the pasta, and feeling loved.

Sung had made new friends, so he was not around much anymore, and as much as that sucked, I understood. My homies always kept me away from the illegal shit, which at the time I resented but also knew that was not me.

I knew some nights they would go out hunting for unlocked cars to steal things and resell them at the swap meet on weekends. Bikes and scooters were also prime targets to sell, and they had big cutters to get through the rope locks. They drove to nefarious places to exchange or buy things for profit. Not something for me—my innocence was obvious and considered a weakness by some.

I would have to leave Dennis's house and sneak back on to Mesa so that I could catch the bus home. I would be so high that I'd forget the time and would have to walk about three miles or so to beat the bus home.

Ramon would always know and wait for me so that I didn't look suspicious.

Security at the high school was tight, but after so many sneaky moments, we had it down to a science. I would wait for the guards to pass by, time my path to the school bus, and when walking toward the stop, act as if I owned the place. Except it didn't work every time.

I had not been jumped or beaten up in a few months going into tenth grade. We were about to go on Christmas break, and I would not see my homies until after the new year. I stayed a little too late at Dennis's the Friday before we started break, drank a few beers I should not have, and smoked entirely too much.

Time skipped by.

Pier and I left together most times, but his house was close, so I walked with him until I had to take my turn onto Fairview. His mom gave me a couple of tamales to go, and they were delicious. It was a dangerous place, and I took the backstreets as best I could, but it didn't matter.

About a half mile from the group home, when I was walking behind the movie theater, a group of young thugs were smoking near a loading dock. They saw me first, and there was nothing I could do before the alarm was shouted.

This was their turf, and I just strolled right up.

I had nothing to give them, was pretty high, and not a fighter. This group looked like they belonged to the Family Mob, a Mexican gang that was well-known around Costa Mesa.

I was in trouble and knew it, so I tried to run. I was not fast and was tackled, with nowhere to go.

"Where are you running, you little *puta*?" one said in a thick Hispanic accent.

"Stop! I am just trying to go home. I am sorry. I didn't know this was your area, and I won't say anything!" I said between getting kicked.

Someone kicked me in the back of the head, and I bit my tongue, spitting out blood. I tried not to blackout from the pain. I felt my eyes water and heard the laughter.

It was happening all over again. They kept kicking me and laughing, calling me names. After a few minutes of not getting kicked, I peeked through my arms. All of them were right back in their loading dock, smoking and staring at me with extreme menace.

They gave me the chance to run, and I did.

I ran all the way to the main street, tasting blood, and I felt a huge lump forming on my head. My homies would never know, and I would never say anything. I recognized a few of the cholos, who had dropped out of high school the year before, and they were not to be messed with.

Surprisingly, two things happened: One, I made it home on time and saw Ramon walking slowly toward the house. "Ramon," I yelled, and he turned around with relief in his eyes.

Two, I saw only Miss Strawberry's car, so if I could get Ramon to distract her, I could run upstairs and get cleaned up.

"What the fuck happened, homie? Who did this? I will fucking kill them!" Ramon said, enraged.

"No, man, let's just get inside, and I will tell you about it later. I don't want Becky to find out," I begged him.

He reluctantly agreed and told me to wait outside but left the door open so I could peek in. Miss Strawberry was in the dining room, and I saw him look out back, pointing. She followed him out to the backyard, and seeing my chance, I ran straight upstairs to the bathroom.

My face looked like shit, and I would not be able to hide the bruising but could at least clean the blood. After changing into clean clothes, it looked like I got punched a few times. There was not much time for anything else, so I grabbed my backpack and got to the kitchen right when they came back inside—mission accomplished.

The start of winter break that year was the first in a long time I knew that seeing my grandfather on Christmas or New Year's would be just a lucky break if it happened.

It didn't.

That year everyone spent Christmas at their daughter Maria's house, and I was the only one at the group home who didn't have family, so it was empty. I remember on Christmas Eve I was asked by the group home parent, Cat Lady, if I would consider staying a few days at the Dover house. That was where kids went who had disciplinary issues.

"Jeremy, I know this is a hard choice, but the staff members and I would like to spend Christmas with our families. Would you be okay spending a little while at the Dover house?" Cat Lady asked genuinely.

Her face had a sadness that I could not get angry at and knew if I said, no she would stay with me over Christmas, which was a horrible thing. "Yeah, I understand, but can I at least have my own room there? Those kids can be really mean, Martha," I said with a fake smile.

Relief blossomed around Cat Lady's face, and she skipped back over to her room. I heard her get on the phone and could feel the happiness in her voice. Kindness will always be the right choice.

One of the staff members from Dover had come to get me in a big blue van that smelled like bologna. He was quiet and not enthused about having to deal with me the day before Christmas.

I didn't get my own room and in fact had to stay in a bay of bunk beds with a group of transient kids. These wayward souls didn't say anything to me, and by the time dinner came around, most had been picked up by family members.

The Dover facility was in Newport Beach, pretty close to the ocean, and was big enough to hold at least fifty kids. From the outside, it looked like a normal business building, with white plaster walls and industrial windows. I had been there once before with the Saint to pick up a kid who ended up staying at the Traverse home.

Christmas 1995 was a reminder of the days at Orangewood.

The coldness of the hospital-like floors flowed through the entire facility, and there was a dark sense of rebellion from those left behind. Call it luck, but the bay in which I bunked had only two others, and they didn't bother me at all.

None of the kids went to Mesa, and they left me alone with my books. That day was like any other, and Dover had minimal staff rotating to share holiday responsibilities. We had pancakes that were pretty good and then were left to our own devices.

Hoping my grandpa would call, I listened for any sound that could be related to a phone ringing, but it was returned as eerie silence. It was not his fault; the family was taking care of him, and I knew he cared about me. I prayed for his health and asked God to protect him.

Christmas was nothing to me. I hated it.

On New Year's, after being back at Dahlia a few days, my grandpa's daughter Maria came to get me for the day, which was amazing. I had missed all of them so much and was hoping this meant I could be with them most weekends following this tough holiday.

School started back up for the last semester of my sophomore year, and I realized quickly my grades were not going to cut it if I wanted to get to the next grade. The intake of pot and ditching had its effect, but they were my best friends, and I decided to choose them over my grades.

My grandfather had no idea I was doing poorly, and I selfishly lied to him, saying everything was fine.

One Sunday, after a movie, he asked me what math I was in, and I didn't tell him why I got kicked out of algebra two.

Toward the beginning of the second quarter of math, I had no idea what we were doing. I would open my textbook to sit facing the teacher but didn't see numbers. Inside the text, I read my fantasy novels, and almost daily the teacher would walk over with a sad smile.

"Jeremy, let me guess," he would say, taking my novel and throwing it out the door.

"Go ahead—get out of my class and follow that book out the door," he said with finality.

I was moved to a remediation math class and felt shameful not telling my grandpa the true story. Instead, I said, "Algebra two, but it's hard for me."

He was an engineer, and I doubt he believed a word I said, but he knew I was a creative and left me alone. Our relationship was always strong, but as I was getting closer to turning sixteen, and not being the good kid I always had been, it showed on the outside.

Bella was more and more likely to stay in the kitchen, not bothering us. She would always be loving and say goodbye when Grandpa drove me home, but I saw the worry on her face. She was scared for him in his vulnerable state, no matter if he denied the pain.

I always had herb with me when I was at his house. I would sneak off to the harbor to smoke a joint, or I brought a glass pipe. He slept a lot and would not notice when I escaped for a little bit, nor talk much if we were both reading in the den. He knew I smoked cigarettes, too, as he caught me smoking in the parking lot with Brett, Bill's oldest grandson. He was eighteen.

Instead of getting angry at me, he just looked at me and then Brett with a bit of annoyance. He lit his own cigarette in the backyard overlooking the lagoon and said to us, "Brett and Jeremy, you don't have to hide smoking from me. Even though I don't approve, I would rather you tell me the truth."

My grandfather's moral code stayed with me, even when I was acting a fool with my homies. They made a lot of shitty choices, and I got made fun of a lot for not agreeing or choosing to not go with them on their crazy adventures.

I started to realize my boys would make fun of me or use me more than I thought was normal. It seemed they knew I needed their friendship more than they needed me around. Noreen loved me and would always protect me when she felt they abused my friendship. She was a mother to us all, so it didn't bother me when they got scolded for hurting me.

We had a dance at our school toward the end of sophomore year, and Martha said I could stay later if I was sure to be out front by eleven thirty. The dance ended at ten, but we never went. Instead, I went with Dennis and our homies to the top of Triangle Square, on the border of Mesa and Newport, to get wasted.

It was stupid and risky, but also the night Noreen gave me the nickname Giggles.

We met friends on the rooftop of the parking structure near Nike Town to drink and smoke pot. We could see if the cops or gang unit were coming from up top, which gave us time to make a break for it.

We didn't get arrested, and after some beers we made it to the bus stop to get home to Dennis's house.

When we walked into their apartment around nine, we were both drunk and high. Noreen was tipsy herself and just looked at us in amusement. "Are you boys wired?" she asked.

We looked at each other and started laughing uncontrollably. We had never heard that saying before. Dennis guided me to the kitchen, where we snacked on delicious food his mom made earlier. We kept laughing about what she said until Dennis asked in a whisper, "Wanna hit the bong before you have to go?"

Not wanting to be weak and knowing it would push me over the edge, I said, "Hell yeah."

I had drunk too much Miller High Life at Triangle Square, and after taking that huge bong rip, I felt the world start to spin. I got the "wa-was."

I could not stay standing, so I lay on the ground in his room, which was a mistake. I felt so nauseous I couldn't get up. Low crawling to the bathroom, I couldn't stop giggling at how stupid I looked. I could hear Dennis laughing, too, which made us both laugh more.

Throwing up was the least of my problems.

I started laughing into the toilet every time I vomited, and it echoed throughout the home. Sweet Noreen knocked on the door and made sure I was okay. She got me to the couch with her and made me drink a lot of water.

"My poor little Giggles. Did Dennis get you all messed up?" she asked sweetly but was staring at her son, who was smiling at us from the hallway.

His smile evaporated quickly, but before he could say anything, I said, "No, never. I chose to do this to myself."

His mom just looked at me with a resigned face and started feeding me bread. I loved her from that moment on more than I thought my heart could. She was an angel and got me reasonably sober before Big Marvin drove me back to the school.

He said, "Jeremy, just don't talk much. And if you have to, say your head hurts really bad from the music."

I thanked him and hugged him goodbye to wait for my pickup, which had not arrived. Trying to make myself presentable, I waited for Cat Lady in silence. Many of the kids around looked at me, knowing I never went to the dance, and just shrugged me off as one of the stoner thugs who ditched all the time.

Cat Lady only asked me how the dance was, and I told her while looking out the window, "The music was too loud, and I feel sick with a headache."

She got me home and didn't bother me about it at all. I was not sure if she believed me but counted my blessings. I knew I smelled of pot.

Mary Jane got me good that night. I also got a funny nickname and became superclose to Dennis's mom. She was another savior whom God put in my path to help protect me from the destruction that was always just a moment away.

I made it through that sophomore year without getting too messed up and had no idea what the next year would bring.

It was not good though.

CHAPTER 26

DEATH

Huntington Harbour, 1996

———————

We die only once, and for such a long time.
—MOLIÈRE

My grandfather died right before Christmas in 1996.

His death came quickly, and it destroyed me. He saved me from myself, and I could not be there for him. He died without seeing me, and a part of me died with him.

Right before his death, I sacrificed my time with him to be with my homies. I lied to his face about what I was doing in school. Those last weekends passed before I realized they were all gone. I should have been with him, not thinking about myself.

There was no more Christmases with the Butlers, and I missed the last one with his family. The way I learned about his death hurt most.

Sunday morning came and went. Sunday afternoon, Maria and her daughters showed up at the Dahlia home. Their eldest daughter, Christina, was tending to Bella while they had to come get me.

I was waiting outside when they drove up, and I knew something was terribly wrong. The girls in the back were defeated and crying. Maria hugged me so hard when I came up to the car, and her eyes were bloodshot.

I knew he was gone. I felt it before and just couldn't believe it. He breathed life into a little boy lost to the world.

"Jeremy, I am so sorry, but Grandpa passed away last night," Maria said as we drove away. She started crying again, and so did the girls in the back.

I had no words. I couldn't believe it as true. I didn't cry, not yet anyway.

I was alone again, with nobody to love me. I didn't say this to the girls. Instead, I held Maria's hand in silent pain. An eternity passed by the time we got to the once bright house I would hardly see again.

The house was dark inside, and I felt lost.

Bella was lying in her bed with tissues all over her floral comforter. I timidly stood by the door, afraid to hear it from her. It was not real; he could still be alive.

"Oh, Jeremy!" she balled with open arms, and I rushed to her side. Bill, his boys, Maria, her girls, Frank Jr, and his wife were all in the room crying. My eyes full of tears, I waited for the words that would take whatever my heart had left.

"He is gone now, Jeremy, but we will always be here," she said.

I just nodded, knowing that was not true. She was breathing hard, and I didn't want to stress her out, so I walked to my grandfather's bedroom.

It still smelled of his aftershave and hair spray.

His closet was open, and the old Hawaiian shirts were still in the same perfect place. Nothing changed. There was a faint smell of cigarettes, and the sun beamed through a slit in the curtains, revealing his made bed. The imprint of him was still there, so I lay in it.

I stayed there for a long time and pretended he was still alive.

My stomach began to knot and ache terribly. I got up to use his bathroom, but Jessica was in the hallway. "Don't worry—I will make sure my mom gets you out of that horrible home," she said, hugging me.

I just nodded and said, "Thanks, Jess. Don't worry about me, okay?"

She looked at me with resignation; I was not a Butler.

I closed the bathroom door, trying to not feel the terrible pain in my gut. Grandpa's shaver was still hanging over the sink, and his hair products were in the open medicine cabinet, flawlessly situated. A faded blue towel hung limply behind the door, and I felt what was left of him. Nobody saw it but me.

I was in his bathroom for an hour and then went outside to get high. Nobody stopped me or noticed. I was not their family, and it was painfully clear on this day.

I walked down to where his old boat was docked, slowly smoking my pipe. The sun was brilliant in the sky, and I felt the salty wind picking up around me. His boat was leisurely rocking in the marina, and I sneaked around the locked gate to sit in his captain's chair.

They would not come here. This was where he and I came to when we wanted to be outside. I smoked a joint, sitting in his seat, thinking of how much I neglected him the past couple of months.

Maria said he had fallen a few days before getting out of his truck and broke his hip. He had trouble healing due to failing kidneys. He made it to the next day, until he could not breathe on his own, and passed away.

Listening to the waves lap against the side of his boat, the wind continued to blow harder, and it felt like nature was saying goodbye to an amazing soul. The earth was sad, and he was no longer in pain. My grandpa had left a beautiful legacy behind.

Finding myself in a lost state, I closed off to the world. I gave up on the debate team and did only enough schoolwork to not fail.

Bella asked if I would speak at his funeral, and I, of course, said yes. I knew exactly what I would say, and it was going to be the hardest thing I had ever done.

The day of his funeral, the wind blew hard. The sun had painted a gorgeous horizon, and most of the trees swayed easily in the wind. Nature knew a force of a man was being honored.

There were huge pine trees all around the church. I felt no fear—just intense emotions. My tears had already started to fall as I walked up to the podium.

"I will miss his voice and his quiet authority. I will miss how much fun we had sneaking into a second movie and how he never complained when I talked nonstop.

"I will miss knowing he was there to protect me from the world I grew up in and how he brought me into his family. I have never felt love like that and hope you have felt it too."

Speaking briefly on our movie escapades, our love of reading, and how losing him would change the entire trajectory of my life gave me a short reprieve from pain. People were crying, and I gave Bella a long hug before walking outside to be alone.

There was no coming back from this. Back at the group home, I knew that was it, and it would be months before I saw Bella, her kids, or grandkids. There was no tomorrow.

Ramon and I went to the gym almost every day to play basketball and watch the Lakers in the locker room. We could stay for hours and walk home since it was close. The little bit of freedom we had we took. It felt good to not think about anything.

One evening, after playing ball for a few hours and even trying to get some tennis in, I met Ron. He was a local swimmer in the gym, who knew everything about baseball. We would talk to him all the time about the Red Sox, his favorite team.

That evening I was feeling particularly down. Ramon didn't come with me, and I decided to just sit by myself in the locker room, watching the Angels. Ron had just finished doing laps and sat next to me in silence.

"You okay? You are always so happy, but you seem down today," he asked with genuine concern. God put someone in my path again to save me from myself.

CHAPTER 27

IRVINE

Irvine, California, 1996–1997

Home is where the heart is.
—PLINY THE ELDER

Echoing sounds of the announcers calling the Angels game combined with the normal locker-room atmosphere faded away like someone turned down the volume knob. Ron's question hit me hard, and my eyes misted over so completely I lost the ability to see. I missed my grandpa and what could have been.

Grandpa epitomized a man with a strong moral compass and gave me hope when there was no hope to give. If God had not graced me with Bob, I would have probably not made it on this earth. Within the deepest corners of my heart, I felt complete sadness and loss.

Ron knew something was wrong, and he asked me, with heartfelt conviction, to explain.

"Jeremy, I have known you a while now. You never are quiet like this, and I can see you are sad. What happened?"

My eyes downcast, I felt tears dropping like mercury meteors onto my basketball shorts and became instantly embarrassed. Controlling my emotions was one of the most difficult internal wars I fought daily. It was impossible, and he was going to think I was just some wimpy little kid.

"It's okay to cry. I am worried about you. What is going on?" Ron asked.

I looked up at him from within my Lakers hoodie and said, "I lost my grandfather, and now I have no one. I am all alone again."

He looked at me with caring eyes.

I looked around, and it was late in the evening, so the locker room was empty. I could hear the pitter-patter of multiple shower heads leaking water on to a cold tile floor.

"What do you mean no one?" he asked.

"I live in group homes, Ron. There is no future for a kid like me out there," I said and pointed toward the outside. My prospects were nil, and my grandfather would be disappointed in my display of giving up. I needed to succeed in life for him but didn't know where to start.

I was not a child anymore; I had just turned sixteen. I had a good head on my shoulders, and God had given me a caring heart, but I was disoriented. Ron looked at me and waited patiently.

His judgment-free approach to talking to me worked over the next few weeks, and he stayed late at the gym with me almost every day. We would talk about group homes, how my mom lost custody and robbed a bank, the death of my father, the death of my grandfather, and the terrible move into the Dahlia home.

Ron never once made me feel bad. In fact, he became angry

that I was treated that way at Dahlia. "Jeremy, are foster homes better?" he asked one day when I was explaining the differences.

That question was loaded, and I could tell from the glint in his eyes. I played along. "Depends on who the foster parent is."

"What if I told you I applied to be your foster dad?" he said, smiling, a twinkle in his blue eyes.

My eyes welled up with tears, and I hid my face.

"Jeremy, I am serious," he said, getting up and patting my shoulder.

I hugged him, not knowing what to say, and he was so surprised he jumped. Even though I was short, I was as tall as him. He hugged me back with a few awkward pats on the back. Ron was not an overtly emotional guy, but I could tell he was happy. He started filling that hole in my heart.

"I will know next week if I am approved, and we can go have lunch or dinner at my home, if you are okay with that."

Walking out of the gym with him, I just nodded and put my Lakers hoodie over my head. I positioned my headphones in my ears and started walking back to Dahlia with a quickened step. This could not be real. This could not be happening to me.

God was watching out for me. My true father. I looked up to the sky with tears streaming down, praying thanks to him. He never let me fall and kept my heart from becoming a black hole of destruction. I was so blessed to have all these great things happen to me.

The next evening at the gym, when we walked out, Ron offered to give me a ride home. I was tired from playing pickup ball for a few hours, and Ramon was with his family in Fountain Valley, so I accepted.

I had never seen his car, but we walked over to a soft yellow Toyota Supra, with a huge spoiler in the back. "This is not your ride, Ron, is it!"

He just smiled and said, "Yes, I am a Porsche guy but fell in love with this car. I am waiting for the new Boxster to come out next year."

I knew cars, especially Japanese streetcars. We all loved them, and I could not wait to tell my homies about this the next day.

He dropped me off a street away so I would not get in trouble and said, "I'll see you next week in the gym."

Walking up to the door, the group home looked different. I knew I would be leaving and believed in Ron.

A few weeks went by, and then Ron came to the group home to tell me his application to be a foster parent was approved. Bella called me to say she had heard from CASA and was scared for me. She realized too late that I was moving on and had felt abandoned by the Butlers.

That was not her fault. Losing Grandpa was devastating and changed everyone in the Butler family. She wanted the best life for me and realized I was left to my own lonely devices, with nobody to provide me the love he once had a bit too late. I would always miss those weekends at their lagoon house in Huntington Beach with my grandpa and my Bella.

I loved Bella, and she came to visit me once after that for lunch to make sure I was okay. She didn't trust Ron and felt like I was making a mistake. I loved her, but I was alone and needed parental love. My mistake would have been to let the Dahlia house think their emancipation program would set me on the path to success.

Ramon and Big Cole were happy for me but felt like they were losing a brother.

Ron came to the group home a few times for in-person hangouts requested by my social worker. He saw the inner workings of the system. That transcended into going to his house for a few hours. He lived in Irvine, a city I never thought I would see. I could not believe a kid like me could be anywhere near his exclusive community.

He lived in Turtle Rock, an affluent neighborhood at the top of a large hill covered in sage, cactus, and immense granite boulders. His two-story house was on the corner, with a massive oak out front that had such ancient limbs they crested low, creating a nest of leafy alcoves. An old-school blue 7 Series Beemer was parked in the driveway, gleaming from a fresh wash. I just stood there, looking around.

A soft breeze played smells like sage and pine and oxygen around my nose. His smile was real as we slowly walked up to the front door of his house, which I was going to call my home. We had stopped by Albertsons at the bottom of the hill to get some shrimp egg rolls. He knew I loved them and heated them up in his awesome convection microwave.

There was a polished grand piano in his sunken living room, which looked out onto a gorgeously maintained yard boasting blooming roses of all colors. Behind that was protected land and seemed to hide his home from the world.

He saw me ogling and said, "That big hill is a great spot to see Fashion Island and the ocean. You can go on up anytime, but be careful—it's a sharp incline."

"I have never seen anything so beautiful," I said simply as he guided me around the house and gave me a tour.

"This is the kitchen and the dining room. Here is the TV room, where I watch too much baseball."

His sitting room had a big TV, a few newspapers, and lots of books. The intricate kitchen had the most unique dark green marble counters I had ever seen.

I saw right then what our connection was. In my backpack, I had the current Piers Anthony Xanth novel I was reading and pulled it out to sit with him. Ron's eyes brightened as we ate our microwaved egg rolls and sat in silence for a few hours just reading. He had baseball going in the background, and I could see the wooden deck outside leading toward those immaculate rose bushes.

"Did you plant those roses?" I asked.

"Many years ago, and they keep coming back more beautiful. Many of the neighbors ask if they can have some, and I let them," he said.

I could tell he took pride in the garden.

I could tell he enjoyed the company and loved that I had a passion for books. It must have been difficult to share a space that had only belonged to him, so I made sure I put everything back as I found it. He had a maid who came twice a week, but I made sure to wipe down the area near that microwave.

Before leaving back to the group home, he showed me his office, which was a Red Sox and Ted Williams tribute room. He had a signed hat and jersey, as well as tons of baseballs in protective cases. The desk was a massive dark oak piece that was covered in paperwork, books, and more Red Sox memorabilia.

Then we walked up a narrow wooden staircase that led to a landing with antique furniture. To the right was my room, and my bathroom was across from that. I had my own bathroom and room; it was too good to be true as I looked out the window of my first personal space.

His master bedroom was beautifully decorated with Tiffany lamps and had a separate suite for his bathroom area. He had another office upstairs dedicated to many of his hobbies, like coding and astrology. He showed me where the laundry area was in the garage and walked through to his Supra.

Driving back to Costa Mesa, I could not understand how this was real. Things were working out, and he said before dropping me off, "Jeremy, we are all set to move you in, and I got approval to be your foster parent."

His eyes were misty, and I knew this was the right thing to do. "When can I leave? I am ready right now," I said, jumping up and down in the Supra.

"We still need to get final approval from South Coast Children's Society, but Kathy seemed so happy for you, and I am not too worried. Maybe we can get you out of there this weekend," he said with a smirk.

I just laughed.

The day he pulled up, I looked at my meager possessions in his trunk, and everything fell into place. Becky and Ramon were there as I walked out of the Dahlia house forever.

I didn't look back as we drove away.

From the age of four to the age of sixteen, I survived group homes and institutions in Southern California. Living with Ron in foster care was a dream come true, and I was not alone anymore. My homeboys were so happy for me, and I had freedom.

Ron never made me stay home, and he never kept unnecessary tabs on me. He knew I was a good kid, and I always told him where I was by leaving notes on the fridge. He even met Noreen and Marvin. Ron let me live my life and gave me the chance to finally be a teenager.

My senior year was going to be awesome, since he was not making me change schools, and he also taught me how to drive his old Beemer. Ron worked every day in Santa Ana, so he could not spend the rest of my junior year driving me to school.

That first night in my room, my selfless foster dad next door and the beautiful night air blowing in from outside, I felt at peace. I belonged, and I was not a group home kid anymore. The void in my heart from losing my grandfather was healing, and when I walked into school the next day, I was free and felt the warmth of the sun on my face again.

It was time to start living.

NORTHERN VIRGINIA

Present Day

Freedom is what you do with what's been done to you.
—JEAN-PAUL SARTRE

The lethargic pitter-patter of spring rainfall outside my home in Northern Virginia brought memories of a time long past. It always did—both good and bad. A time when rare summer rain kept us indoors at Orangewood and away from the awful bullying. Rain that splashed huge droplets onto the dark sapphire surface of my grandfather's lagoon and reminded me of boiling pasta water. Those memories kept me grounded.

I wanted to feel the rain on my skin, so I opened the white balcony doors off our master bedroom and looked out to a beautiful backyard that felt complete. Cool air touched my much-older face, and the steely clouds were so low in the sky I could feel their atmosphere. It smelled of the fresh pine and holly trees planted last year that made our home an oasis we never wanted to leave. The dimmed sun was hoping to breakthrough, but the cleansing rain was not done nourishing our world.

"How did I get here?" I asked myself out loud while breathing in the crisp freedom I never knew could be real.

After an interesting couple of years in foster care and some increasingly bad times with friends, I made the difficult choice to leave everything I knew or cared about behind. A new journey in the military was a perfect recipe to add to my fight of never being like my mother. It was the best decision I could have made, and the navy gave me a powerful platform to succeed. Everywhere I went, I carried the power of surviving group homes close to my heart like a God-blessed bulletproof set of impenetrable armor.

Anytime life became hard to bear, I remembered what I survived. That invisible mantle of strength became the stepping stone for a way of living that centered on never giving up. I made many mistakes along the path to today but never forgot that even the most stabbing of pain shall pass. Even during the hardest moments of my divorce or losing my precious kids or difficult hours worked in the Middle East, I felt the familiar touch of survival harden my spine.

Today I have been blessed beyond anything I could have imagined. There were many moments when I thought jail was the next stop, or I would barely make it from one dead-end job to another. Life seemed hopeless. Group home kids are survivors and deserve a chance to prove themselves. They need to see how strong they are for winning even one day in the system, let alone a young lifetime.

Help me get this message out there to those in need. To those living alone in an institution, in a broken family, within a deplorable facility, or in an abusive household. Never give up on yourself, and remember: resiliency is your superpower.

STAY RESILIENT,

JB

ABOUT THE AUTHOR

Jeremy Bracamontes survived group homes all around Orange County, California, from age five until he joined the Navy as a cryptologic technician at nineteen. He has a master's degree in cyber security from The George Washington University.

After serving, Jeremy was employed as a federal contractor with multiple deployments to Iraq and Afghanistan supporting special operations. He then moved into leadership roles providing strategic business development to both large and small defense contracting firms around DC.

He lives in Northern Virginia with his wife and children. Jeremy's wife pushed him to write this memoir to help good kids who have struggled and for his family to understand the hardships endured.

GLOSSARY

Adoption. Dream mode initiated. This path is a ward of the courts dream come true, be it in a community center, group home, or foster home. It is just a dream though. The reality is, adoption rarely comes for children over the age of six or so; infants are what people want, and that is fair. Sometimes a volunteer, advocate, or big brother or sister will foster and finally adopt the ward they cared for, but that's not a normal situation. Many times, the abusive mother or father will not give up parental rights. This makes the child ineligible, and then time takes over.

Foster Homes. The most used and least understood home a ward of the court occupies. Oversimplified in movies or books, the foster home is where most group home kids dream of. In many situations, the foster child lives with a few other kids in a loving environment and will go to school like everyone else. It is easy to hide foster home life at school, but everyone knows who the group home kid is. Not to be taken lightly, this home is often temporary. There are some foster homes that strive to give kids a better life and teach them to become great adults, but there are also some that are devious in their attempt to take money from the state. In rare situations, one can find a foster home with seven or more kids piled into a small house, and the intent is for the foster parent to collect that monthly stipend from the government. Disgusting.

Immediate Shelter Homes (ISH)/Temporary Care. With a moment's notice, willing to accept a poor, innocent child into your home and care for them like they are your own—that is an ISH. Most times the setting is a foster home, and in some winning circumstances the child placed temporarily become permanent. This is rare. The child is torn from an abusive home, and the community facilities or nearby group homes have no vacancy, so where do these little souls go? A child can stay anywhere from one night to multiple months, but in most cases it's simply a waypoint to Orangewood.

Group Homes. What could be the most traumatic of homes, it is where children reside who have been taken from their families, based on the actions of the parents or the difficulties of the child. Group homes, also known as six-bed facilities, are based on the sleeping arrangements allowed per home. In most cases, this is six, and they almost always have one for boys and one for girls, if not more. These homes are also broken out by degree of difficulty and age.

Six-Bed Facility/High-Risk Emotionally Neglected. Innocence is hard to keep, and some situations in life take it away without permission. In a group home, it's impossible to see the world as a "normal" kid. It's even harder if the child has been emotionally abused or neglected. Trust is gone, and the light of innocence, so beautiful to witness in a child's eyes, has been clouded over. They have either been painfully taken from their families directly or temporarily housed in a community youth facility, like Orangewood Children's Foundation. Either way, there is extreme emotional trauma to diagnose and treat. Even the well-trained psychological staff at these homes can't handle certain cases.

Six-Bed Facility/Low-Risk Emotionally Neglected. Same as above, but these neglected children might be a bit older, have been in group homes longer, or had advocates with them. An example is the court-appointed special advocate (CASA) program, which gave those sweet, innocent children someone to share love and friendship with. This love, which is needed to start emotional healing, was withheld from the high-risk home, based on the child potentially running away or becoming physically violent. Children here are normally well behaved, develop a stronger sense of consequence, and have family or advocates who take them for the weekend. More leniency is granted in the ways of freedom from the house and staying later at school.

Group Home/High-Risk Developmentally Disabled. Although broken out by gender and age, the goal of these facilities is to help those who can't help themselves. These children were victims of drug or alcohol many times during pregnancy and did not properly develop. This led to extreme developmentally disabled injuries that need 24-7 care. Some situations stem from a violent parent who hurts the child to the point of disability. Many of these children are sweet and innocent; they are victims of child abuse.

Group Home/High-Risk Physically Disabled. This is hero work, and the staff members who dedicate their lives to helping these poor children are the most selfless, amazing people. It is hard, thankless work taking care of children who can't walk, talk, or even move, but these heroes do it. A group home such as this is humbling for staff and volunteers.

Group Home/Low-Risk Developmentally Disabled. Isolating and quiet, these homes are tailored for hypersensitive children. Children could be high-functioning or low-functioning autistic or have disabilities like Down syndrome. These homes were separated by age and gender due to their higher cognitive abilities.

Group Home/Low-Risk Physically Disabled. Sometimes a child moved to and from these homes due to their physical abilities not being permanent. Unfortunately, there are some children who, at no fault of their own, have permanent physical deformities or conditions that make it very difficult to be in public. The children in these homes are especially strong. They have mental fortitude, even with physical ailments.

Group Home/Detention Center. There are no age limits here. Essentially, the detention facility uses an expanded group home model to create a larger facility with the primary objective of controlling children who are simply uncontrollable and could become a risk in public or to the public. Violence, defiance to authority, and extreme rage are some of the mainstays here. For some low-risk kids, there are no other choices, and although a transient location, they can leave lasting impressions.

Group Home/Emancipation Facility. Fear and sadness radiate from group home kids who have matured and are required to relocate to a cold world where expectations stem from getting a job, volunteer work, and earning all their privileges. The idea of this facility is better than the actual emancipation practice. The home does not prepare children for the real world or how to not be a "group home kid." The school and group home can help the kids find work, but only for those who are trusted. If the kid came from a detention facility still hosting darkness, it was unlikely they could hold a job or want one, for that matter. A hierarchy is formed in these homes, usually with a punch to the face. Size matters, and it's usually the biggest, meanest kid who thrives as a bully and enjoys causing pain in a way that takes over his or her poor life. Many of the emancipated children strive more for gangs, and that is hard to dispute, as that is where they feel like family. Their trajectory is not where one should want to head.

Group Home/Adult Care. Like the high-risk homes, many children remain in a childlike state of mind and can't function in public without supervision. Their developmental disabilities or physical disabilities (or both), based on abusive and neglecting parents, forever change the way these super sweet kids become adults—they don't.

Community Youth Facility/Orphanage. Terror pulls at the very
lining of a child's life in these facilities. Imagine the hour before
eating dinner with your family and the next being stripped
down to go through a prisonlike entrance procedure at what
essentially is an orphanage. A community youth facility is broken down by age groups, sex, and each location is called a ward.
For example, boys between the age of six and twelve reside in
the preteen ward that is directly across from the girls' ward.
From infant to the age of emancipation, these places have hundreds of kids. The other side of the coin is that many of the
children are put there by the parents or psychologists based on
their inability to discipline. With some kids, an intervention is
required, and places like Orangewood are willing to introduce
a prisonlike structure behind walls you can't get out of. Talk
about a jump back to reality. These kids are usually the ones who
torment the innocent and bully their way to the top of the food
chain. In an orphanage you learn the value of silence, the value
of fear and how to hide.

Juvenile Hall/Detention Facility. Thuggish mentality is the entrance
fee. Sometimes the juvie kid is wrongfully accused or takes the
hit for someone by not ratting. Yet violent, angry, abusive bullies
reign here and enjoy hurting others. Not hard to hide, these emotionally and many times physically abused kids lash out in very
illegal ways. Group home kids find an easy path to juvie.

Jail/Prison (Minor tried as an adult). The neglect and abuse are
too much for some poor kids. They are unable to come back and

end up committing terrible crimes. Crimes where they are tried as adults, and sometimes this occurs when they are in a group home or community center. There is no point in talking about the crimes themselves here—just devastating.

Group Home Staffing

1. **Group Home Business Owner:** CEO/president of a group home business.
2. **Group Home Business Leadership:** C-suite and executive-level group home personnel.
3. **Group Home Psychiatric Leadership:** Collective of clinical MDs and PHDs.
4. **Group Home Parent:** Resides at the home, hires personnel, orders goods, and is on call.
5. **Senior Staff Member:** In charge of staff members, daily operations, and procedures.
6. **Morning Staff:** In charge of waking, feeding, and organizing for school in the morning.
7. **Day Staff:** On call when kids arrive from school; runs the afternoon and evening routines.
8. **Night Staff:** Minimal staffing at night. One staff member in charge of nightly routines.
9. **Weekend Staff:** Full staffing routines all day; three kids per monitoring staff member.
10. **Advocate/Volunteers:** CASA or other volunteer groups who take kids out for enjoyment.
11. **Security Personnel:** On-call personnel to handle altercations, violence, and runaways.

12. **Social Worker:** Weekly guidance leader and emotional health expert who is also on call.

13. **Therapist:** Holds weekly therapy sessions with the whole group home as a collective.

14. **Psychologist:** Monthly private therapy sessions to help with emotional trauma and neglect.

15. **Psychiatrist:** Quarterly private therapy sessions focused on mental and emotional health.